Yes, we are of good courage, a
the body and at home with the Lord. So whether we are at
home or away, we make it our aim to please him.
—2 Corinthians 5:8–9 (ESV)

Dear Reader,

MR LAWRENCE THOMPSON
PO BOX 8798
ERIE PA 16505-0798

There is undeniable comfort in realizing God's promises are true. Heaven is a glorious place, our final destination. It is a real place where we will find peace one day. There are a few people who have been given the unimaginable gift of seeing heaven before it becomes their everlasting home. Valerie Paters was one of those who through an extraordinary set of circumstances discovered the immeasurable peace of God's glory when she journeyed to heaven and back.

It was a welcome departure from the cares of this world, and like others who have embraced this experience, she longed to return to heaven. Her return to this life, however, was the result of an obedient prayer from her sister Cheryl Schuelke. Upon receiving a word from God and a vision of her sister's heavenly experience, she prayed in the hospital room where her sister's body lay until that moment when she finally opened her eyes. It's the type of story *Guideposts* is known for. Sharing through other people's experiences the power of hope, the promise of prayer, and the value of trusting in the goodness and mercy of God is a part of the *Guideposts* tradition.

Heaven Is a Breath Away will take you on the remarkable spiritual journey of these two sisters who overcame pain and loss on their way to discovering God's purpose for their lives. From wrestling with insecurities during childhood to Valerie's horrific accident that transformed their perception of and relationship with heaven, they come to relish the supreme comfort of God's love and realize how close heaven really is.

Also, at the end of this book you'll get the bonus of another amazing, true *Guideposts* story that will inspire your faith. "A Mother's Hope" by Tiffini Dingman-Grover is the story of a woman who, like Cheryl, was determined not to say good-bye to her loved one as he faced death. She, too, turned to prayer, doing so diligently in her son's hospital room, holding on to the belief that her child's journey to heaven wouldn't last.

Life as we know it is a precious gift, and it is a brief part of our spiritual journey. Beyond this world is another—our final destination—filled with God's grace and love. It's a place Valerie and Cheryl have discovered and still long for. As they share their story, be comforted, strengthened, and filled with hope as you read of the heavenly home—a real place, magnificent in scope and beauty, permeated with iridescence, and alive with divine energy—that awaits us when we draw our last breaths here on earth. And you'll see more clearly than ever that God is always present, His love is overflowing, and His promise of heaven is real!

Faithfully yours,
Editors of Guideposts

HEAVEN IS A BREATH AWAY

*An Unexpected Journey
to Heaven and Back*

Valerie Paters and Cheryl Schuelke
with Kay Farish

Guideposts
New York

This Guideposts edition is published by special arrangement with Morgan James Publishing.

Heaven Is a Breath Away
An Unexpected Journey to Heaven and Back

Unless otherwise identified, all directly quoted Scriptures are taken from The Holy Bible: English Standard Version, copyright © 2001, Wheaton: Good News Publishers. Used by permission. All rights reserved.

Published in New York, New York, by Morgan James Publishing. Morgan James and The Entrepreneurial Publisher are trademarks of Morgan James, LLC. www.MorganJamesPublishing.com

The Morgan James Speakers Group can bring authors to your live event. For more information or to book an event visit The Morgan James Speakers Group at www.TheMorganJamesSpeakersGroup.com.

ISBN   9781630473044   paperback
ISBN   9781630473051   eBook
ISBN   9781630473068   hardcover
Library of Congress Control Number:
2014942203

Interior Design by:
Chris Treccani
www.3dogdesign.net

DEDICATIONS

From Valerie:

To my sister, Cheryl Schuelke, and brother-in-law, Dave, for their continued strength and support

To my daughters, Elissa and Ashley, whom I love with all my heart

To my granddaughters, Ariel, Olivia, and Lillian—all three of you are precious treasures.

From Cheryl:

To my husband, Dave, who encourages, supports, and releases me to do all the Lord has called me to do. You are my best friend and the love of my life! I love you!

To my children, Shannon, David (Tamara), and Daniel (Janessa)—you are my gifts from God!

To my granddaughter, Aleia—you are Nana's delight.

From Valerie and Cheryl:

Thank you to our Bridegroom, King Jesus, who will forever be revealing to us the wonders of His love.

To our parents, whom we love and honor.

To our baby sister—we love you.

To Aunt Julie, who knows the great pain of losing three daughters—this is for you. We love you.

To Aunt Violeta (Boo)—you are an example of one who has endured many trials with faith, strength, and joy and has overcome!

ACKNOWLEDGMENTS

To our dear friends, John and Deb Rusk—thank you for your wise counsel, prayer, and support. It is a privilege and honor to be in ministry with you. The best is yet to come.

To Pastor Scott and Lydia Ingegneri and our Grace North Church family who have welcomed us with open arms and are cheering us on—we love you!

To Pastor Jack and Jane Lankhorst who saw the gift of prophetic intercession, and trained, equipped, and released us—we will be forever grateful!

To our friends and team of intercessors, Tamara Schuelke, Mary Sheppard, Sharri Martin, Anne Raczkowski, Sandy Whicker, and countless others, too many to mention. You know who you are. Thank you for the years of dedicated prayer not only on this book but the many assignments the Lord has given us together in the prayer closet. His kingdom come! On Earth, as it is in heaven!

To Kay Farish, our friend and writer— thank you for the many hours you sacrificed to help us get our story out.

To Janice VanCronkhite, thank you for your exquisite prophetic artwork for this book cover. God painted a beautiful picture through you. We encourage others to visit your web site at www.jvcartworks.com.

To Donna Scuderi, we know you were a godsend. His timing is perfect. Thank you for editing our book.

To Patty Brudeseth, thank you for your input and time spent reading our book, over and over.

CONTENTS

Foreword   XI

A Note from Valerie   XV

1. The Unexpected and the Ordinary   1

2. Something in the Rearview Mirror   13

3. Steps toward Heaven   33

4. From One Life to the Next   49

5. Two Different Worlds   69

6. The Broken Body and the Blessings   83

7. Light Overcoming Darkness   95

8. One Step at a Time   105

9. To Each a Path   125

10. Memories and Miracles   135

11. New Horizons   151

12. His Purposes, His Bride   177

13. A Beautiful Story   187

Afterword: The Book   195

Afterglow   200

A Mother's Hope by Tiffini Dingman-Grover   202

FOREWORD

To say that something is life-changing is often an overstatement. However, it applies to *Heaven Is a Breath Away*. I should know. I was an eyewitness to the events of this amazing story, and my life was deeply changed by it.

To heaven and back is Valerie's story. It includes the massive accident that took her life; it also includes her time in heaven and her return here as a modern-day Lazarus. She came back with a message. She *is* a message from God so vitally needed by this generation.

If you listen with an open heart, perhaps you'll recognize that Valerie's story is not very different from your own. Who is this God we believe in and what is He really like? And what about heaven, and how does it relate to current life with all its miseries? Does Jesus really love us?

Valerie's story will answer these questions, and more, if you let it.

Her sister Cheryl's story intertwines beautifully with Valerie's, giving revelation of the dynamic possibilities of an intimate relationship with God that both understands what God wants to do in the crisis *and* faithfully prays it into existence. Cheryl and the many who interceded for Valerie model for us what it means to pray the Father's heavenly will down into this earthly realm. To be the friend of God—one who knows the divine heart and who lives the life of answered prayers—is open to all who would pursue it. Cheryl's story affirms the potential of living the Spirit-filled life in tune with the Father.

As you journey through this double-perspective story with Valerie and Cheryl, be alert for spiritual insights, for they are many. Among them are the following:

- Life here is fragile and your time can come suddenly. Are you ready?

- Heaven is a real place, a real destiny for those who love Him. Are you going there?

- Jesus really is who He said He is and He has a place for you. He knows you and truly loves you.

- God speaks to us, if we will listen. He is a God of revelation.

- God answers persistent, Spirit-directed prayer. Therefore all things are possible to the person who believes.

Finally, and central to this whole story, Jesus has a people called the Church, His Bride whom He is laboring to heal and prepare to be with Him. He wants us all to be in it and to be made whole. As a living metaphor, that is the message Jesus sent Valerie back from heaven to declare! Jesus is preparing the Bride whom He loves. What is broken can be mended. What is damaged can be healed. What is dirty can be cleansed. What is dead can be made alive.

The time is short; behold He is coming soon! The Spirit and the Bride say, "Come!" Let the Bride make herself ready, for heaven is a breath away.

—Pastor John Leon Rusk

The Frontlines Ministries, www.thefrontlines.org
www.patmosontheplains.com

A Note from Valerie

On a snowy Arizona day in the year 2000 my life changed forever. Two semis crashed into my stopped Jeep Cherokee, trapping me beneath another huge truck that was parked on the shoulder, waiting out the blizzard.

Upon impact, my daughter was thrown from the car, sustaining moderate injuries. My fate was more horrific. It took hours for first responders to extricate me and rush me to the hospital. Once there, I was placed on life support and declared ventilator dependent.

For three days I was "not there"; I was with Jesus, in heaven. This book is about the joys and wonder of that journey. As you read it, I pray you will enter His presence, sense His love and power, and be drawn by His compassion. I want you to hope for heaven. It is real and waiting for those who believe in Jesus. He wants to welcome you with open arms to a paradise so rich I can barely put it into words.

Know that Cheryl and I are praying for you as you read these pages. We have laid our lives bare in the hope that you will see how good God is. We have also written about others. To protect them, many names have been changed. There are, however, no composite people in this book. All of the events actually happened. Details of the accident and my time in the hospital are verified and documented. Not everyone is mentioned—only those whose role is essential in telling the story.

As you travel to heaven and back with me, may you be blessed, encouraged, and forever changed, as I was.

> *Yes, we are of good courage, and we would rather be away from the body and at home with the Lord. So whether we are at home or away, we make it our aim to please Him (2 Corinthians 5: 8-9 ESV).*

—**Valerie Paters**

The Unexpected and the Ordinary

At almost three in the afternoon on March 20th, a big black semi barreled into Flagstaff, Arizona. Snow was mixing with light rain as the driver slowed for traffic merging on approach to an off-ramp for US 89A.

The weather wasn't unusual for that time of year. Roads were only slightly slick and visibility was good, so the truck driver didn't expect the silver Jeep Cherokee parked on the right a couple of miles ahead. He didn't even see the blinding snow until it dropped like a curtain about a hundred yards in front of his rig.

Another semi was parked on the right shoulder. Cars were slowing in the middle and left lanes. The Jeep wasn't moving but the big black truck was. With all his might the trucker pumped his squealing brakes. The wheels caught the icy pavement and slipped, jerking the trailer to the right as the cab veered left. He tried desperately to avoid the Jeep, but his rig headed fast for it. He'd lost control, and with a mind of its own, his semi roared into the silver car.

The impact sounded like a bomb going off.

Before the trucker had time to think, the red cab of another semi hurtled toward him as a propane truck slowed in the far left. The jackknifed rig stuck out into the middle lane. All the trucker could do was clutch the steering wheel and wait for the red semi to plow into him.

Metal flew everywhere as the oncoming truck devoured everything in its path. Its load swerved back and forth like the tail of a dragon, throwing cars into ditches and knocking the propane tank sideways. Behind the second big rig, cars piled up or flew off the roadway. It sounded like a war zone. Snow was hurled upward as vehicles dove and landed in ravines along the route's edge.

An eerie quiet descended. The trucker was trapped in his rig and badly shaken. He couldn't see the red truck or the Jeep. The cab of his truck was smashed into the parked semi. His load pushed into the back of it, creating a small, icy triangle of pavement.

There, in the triangle, lay a girl who wasn't moving.

Accident scene: Valerie's Jeep Cherokee beneath two semis—only the rear tire on driver's side is visible.

Valerie's car at the wrecking yard

A Day in the Life

Earlier that morning, Valerie Paters drove to the Flagstaff Mall tax office where she was a tax preparer. The brunette worked with her sister Cheryl during the tax season. The two had always been close, but now Valerie was preoccupied and in turmoil. Her thoughts weighed on her as she entered the office, swung her coat over the rack, and went to the kitchen to make coffee. The forty-year-old mother of two yawned and put a filter into its plastic cone.

Arriving coworkers were greeted by fresh coffee and a ringing phone. "Hello. H and R Block. How may I help you?"

The receptionist was speaking with Cheryl. Valerie could hear her sister's deep, rich laugh. She expected Cheryl to ask for her, but she didn't. Valerie knew her sister was worried. *I wish I knew how to let her know what's going on inside of me. I can't put it into words. How can I make sense of it for her when it doesn't make sense to me?*

The phones rang more steadily and clients arrived for their appointments. The busyness made time pass quickly, and lunchtime arrived before Valerie knew it. She looked forward to walking the mall each day, saying hello and joking around with friends in nearby shops. Her small talk was never too serious. Valerie Pater's specialty was making people laugh.

At around two o'clock Valerie cleaned up her desk. It was time to pick up her younger daughter, Ashley, from middle school before traffic got snarled. Meanwhile, her daughter Elissa arrived from school with a change of clothes over her arm.

"Hi, Mom," she called out to Valerie as she breezed toward the restroom.

Elissa worked the office phones in the evenings, and Valerie was proud of how her older daughter handled herself. As Valerie slipped into her coat, Elissa emerged from the restroom, dressed for work. She set her things on a desk and asked, "You off to pick up Ashley?"

"Yes," Valerie answered, smiling. "See you tonight."

As she passed Elissa, Valerie planted a kiss on her cheek.

"Not in public, Mom," scolded her daughter, only half kidding.

"I'll kiss you when I want," Valerie said with a smile as she rummaged through her purse for her car keys.

"Be careful out there, Mom," warned Elissa. "I heard it's getting icy on the freeway already."

"Okay," Valerie called back. Then she walked out the door.

Her daughters were on her mind as she headed for the mall exit. Tomorrow was Ashley's fourteenth birthday. Valerie couldn't believe so many years had passed since her baby's birth. She could not imagine what she would do without her girls. They made her difficult marriage bearable.

When Valerie reached her car, it was coated with snow. She slipped into the driver's seat and slid the key into the ignition.

～

That morning, Ashley popped out of bed without being told. She could hardly wait to wear one of the five new outfits her mother had bought her on Saturday. Tomorrow she would be fourteen. Soon she would be old enough to drive and date. And next year she'd be in high school.

Ashley brushed her teeth, pulled her hair into a ponytail, and spread her new clothes across her bed: two skirts, four tops, three pairs of jeans, and a jacket. It was going to be really cold that day, so she chose the jacket and dark gray V-necked sweater. Then she held up the short black skirt. *Nah. I'd have to wear tights with that.* The rhinestone-studded jeans would be better. Ashley took the outfit and left the rest of the clothes on the bed.

In the shower she thought about how to celebrate her birthday on Tuesday. Her mom asked where she'd like to eat. It would just depend on how she felt when the time came. Maybe Mexican food. Or Italian. It might be fun to invite a friend, too. She probably wouldn't choose any of the girls from church, though. Her mom would like that, but Ashley didn't feel like she fit in with the "perfect" kids. They were too religious for her taste. She went to church because she loved her mom and liked the worship music. Yeah, church was okay. But Ashley knew she'd never be the religious type. Too many rules and too much judgment.

"You look cute," said Valerie as they hopped in the Jeep. "I like that outfit on you."

"Thanks, Mom. It's pretty cold already, huh?" Ashley shivered.

"It's supposed to snow this afternoon," Valerie said, backing down the driveway as Ashley turned on the radio.

As usual, the school day dragged on for Ashley. Looking out the window of her sixth-period class, she saw snow falling in large flakes. Between the snow and the drone of her teacher's voice, concentration was impossible. Watching the athletic field turn to cotton fluff was much more interesting.

Into the Blizzard

When the final bell rang, Ashley grabbed her books and walked in the snow to Aunt Cheryl's house a couple of blocks away. The wind swirled in little cyclones as icy flakes stung Ashley's cheeks. She hadn't gotten very far when she heard her mom's Jeep crunching the snow.

"Get in, Ashley," said Valerie, reaching across to open the passenger door. "And hurry up. The heater's on."

"Okay, Mom." Ashley brushed snowflakes from her jacket collar. "You're on time."

"Yeah. I want to get home before the traffic gets crazy. You know how the freeway is when it snows."

Ashley rubbed her hands together. "Brrr," she said, and popped a 4Him album into the car stereo. As her mom drove onto the I-40 ramp, Ashley sang along with her favorite Christian song, "In His Care."

Slowly, Valerie merged into westbound traffic and passed several big rigs. Ashley noticed the trucks, including the last one—a big, black Peterbilt. She thought, *Hmmm. Lots of trucks on the road today.*

Suddenly the snow became a blizzard. Traffic slowed and brake lights flashed. *Probably a wreck up ahead.* Ashley couldn't see two feet in front of her. Valerie pumped the brakes to keep from skidding off the freeway. The Jeep came to a stop in the right lane next to a white semi parked on the shoulder.

"We should be okay right here," said Valerie. She shifted the car into park and looked at Ashley.

That was all she had time to do. Ashley glanced in her side-view mirror and saw a black rig careening toward them. It was the Peterbilt.

"Jesus!"

Sister Love

Cheryl Schuelke had the day off—comfy sweats, no makeup, hair bunched into a silver claw. Instead of enjoying her time off from the tax office, she tried to shake the nagging unease she'd felt since waking up.

Around ten in the morning Cheryl called the office to see how things were going. She usually spoke with Valerie, but for some reason hadn't today. It was weird not hearing her sister's voice, but she figured she would catch up with her later on.

The sisters had prayed with others at Canyon Chapel Church every Thursday morning for well over a year. The group was tightly knit and very transparent with each other. But for the past few months, Valerie had distanced herself, as though navigating a world of her own. Cheryl thought, *If only she would talk about what was going on.*

At about 2 p.m. the snow began falling, lightly at first. As it blanketed the lawn, Cheryl tried straightening the house, and then switched to reading. She couldn't seem to focus on anything for more than a few minutes, so she watched the heavy snowflakes plummet to the ground.

Still, she was uneasy. So she prayed.

Late in the day, her phone rang. It was Elissa. "Aunt Cheryl, they closed Interstate 40 and I can't get in touch with Mom." Her voice was anxious. "There's been an accident on the freeway, and I can't get a hold of Mom."

Valerie had recently purchased a cell phone for just this purpose. Something caught in Cheryl's chest as she tried to remember… it seemed like she'd done this before. She brushed off the feeling.

"Maybe you have the wrong number." Cheryl knew accidents in bad weather could tie up the freeways for hours. "What number did you call?"

When Elissa repeated the number, it was wrong. *Thank God.* Cheryl drew a deep breath. "You have the wrong number," she said, and almost laughed with relief.

After the call Cheryl flipped on the television. Channel 3 was reporting on the wreck. "There is a multicar pileup on I-40. There are injuries, but that is all we know at this time. Stay tuned for continuing coverage."

The dispassionate report grated against the intuition still stirring inside. Cheryl turned off the television and tried to quell the foreboding. Then she dialed Valerie's cell phone and dreaded that she might not pick up.

She didn't.

Sunday Morning

Valerie

On the Sunday morning before the wreck, I rolled over in bed to find the empty place beside me already cold. The man I'd married twice was an early riser. Brian was either at work or in the garage. I rubbed my arms to ward off the chill. Flagstaff is cold in March. I should have been used to it, but I was irritated by it. So I padded to the closet for my robe and slippers, and then slogged to the kitchen.

The cold wasn't the issue. Being irritated had become the norm for me. All the emotions I used to override were surfacing, and I didn't like it. I had gotten pretty good at the façade. Being the life of every party, joking around, and laughing had worked for years—but not anymore.

Ever since I was a kid, my jokes were mostly self-deprecating. Until recently I'd never wondered why. But something shifted during the final months of 1999, and I couldn't seem to cope. It first showed up in the intercessors' group. After prayer we'd eat together and talk. I used to look forward to it, but now I just wanted to be left alone. Any excuse to avoid the women would do. They wanted to talk and pray about a relationship with God that I wasn't ready for.

That Sunday before service, I was to meet the group and pray as we always did. My stomach tightened. It all seemed too intimate, like God was prying into places I didn't want Him to go. I felt fragile and quick to cry. The old ways of handling my feelings weren't working for me.

Ashley and I went to church together. When I entered the prayer room, I barely glanced at Cheryl. She could read me like a book, and I wanted to avoid any heavy conversations. My emotions were too raw for that.

Our pastor, John Rusk, soon came in and asked us to wrap up the meeting so another group could use the room. Relieved, I rushed out without Cheryl and slipped into a back row where I could sit, quiet and unnoticed.

Cheryl

When Valerie arrived at pre-service prayer on March 19th, she looked like she'd been crying. Just as she appeared, our pastor asked us to make way for the Sunday school class. There was no time to talk to Valerie or even pray for her. But during the service

I watched my sister. She was not herself. The light was gone from her eyes. She was wrestling with something heavy, but I didn't know what.

Midway through the service, I ran to the restroom and burst into tears. *What is this I'm feeling, Lord? What is Valerie struggling with?* There was no specific answer, so I blew my nose, fixed my mascara, and tiptoed back into the sanctuary.

One thing I knew for sure: ever since the surgeries Valerie had as a little girl, her life had been difficult. That was such a long time ago. But maybe her childhood struggles were only now taking their toll.

2

SOMETHING IN THE REARVIEW MIRROR

That Sunday evening, Pastor John and his wife held a potluck supper at their home. Cheryl arrived in time to see Valerie and Ashley walk toward the pastor's door. Again, tears streaked Cheryl's cheeks. *What is this heaviness I'm sensing, Lord? What is going on with Valerie?*

Valerie was quiet during dinner. Cheryl wanted to talk to her, but didn't know what to say. Her sister was viewing life through a different lens. Surely, it must have everything to do with the past.

Long Ago Reflections

Valerie

Ashley and I arrived at the pastor's potluck just before Cheryl did. I was still in "quiet mode," so we didn't talk much. Brian was supposed to come, but didn't. I wished that were different. Somehow I felt that it reflected on me.

The bigger issue was the mirror I saw myself in. It was flawed. I know that now. But on that Sunday evening I was still feeling *less than*. The foot operations, the handicapped school, the teasing and weird looks from other kids, plus the wheelchairs, crutches, and unanswered prayers for healing—I never seemed to measure up.

Even at seven, I knew that God couldn't really love me. I was *less than* and had trouble walking. No one knew that I had familial muscular dystrophy, a disorder affecting the primary muscles. There was no definitive diagnosis at the time, so I had several surgeries throughout my childhood.

The operations left me unable to go to public school. So when I was eight, I started at the "special" school. With my pink polka-dot dress and matching hair ribbon, I felt out of place. This wasn't like last year's school. Those kids acted like most kids do. These kids had severe disabilities, and some of them were in wheelchairs. They were dealing with more than I was—more than just having casts on their feet. And instead of one teacher per classroom, this school had a teacher and an aide helping some students do ordinary stuff, like eating.

Why am I here? I can eat. I can read and sing and write and draw, too!

"And you must be Valerie," a nice lady said while pushing my wheelchair to her desk. "We are glad to have you here at Saint Lawrence School."

She left off *for the Handicapped*. Not that I knew exactly what that meant.

"Let's see how well you read," the teacher said as she pulled a small red book from the shelf. "Here."

Before I knew it, the book was in my hands. It made me so nervous, I wasn't sure I could read anymore.

"Go on," said the nice lady. "Try."

The book was about a big dog. I flipped it open, and read.

Whew!

My new school was mostly set up like any regular school. The children were disabled, but they functioned. Unlike my former school, everyone here accepted everyone else. Yet, my mind said this was a place for throwaways. If your parents were ashamed of you, this was where you went.

∼

The problem was my feet. They didn't work right and made walking difficult. Mom and Dad took me to doctor after doctor. I listened as they discussed me using words I didn't recognize. Yet I understood: my body wasn't like other kids' bodies. Mine was different. Physically I could not keep up with "normal" kids. So I chose not to play outside with them.

"Surgery," said one last physician. "That is our only recourse."

Before my first operation, Mom made a suggestion as we drove home from the doctor's office. "We could call Pastor Rowlette,

Dean. See if the elders of the church will pray for Valerie before she goes to the hospital."

Dad nodded slowly. "Yes…yes, we could." He took a deep breath. "Probably a good idea, Frances."

When I looked into the rearview mirror from the back seat, I saw my father's face. *Is he mad at me, or just thinking?* I couldn't help feeling that my feet were making a mess of everything.

The next evening, I sat surrounded by men who placed their hands on my head. "Heal this child of Yours, in the name of Jesus!" they prayed. "Heal her for Your glory, Jesus!"

The men prayed hard for me. But the next morning, I still went for surgery. For some reason, Jesus didn't want to make me better. *That must be the answer.* A seed of shame dropped into my soul and settled deep down.

The morning after my surgery, I awoke with my feet in casts and pain shooting up my legs as though someone had stuck swords in my heels. The slightest movement sent shockwaves through my body. Mom and Dad caressed me, prayed over me, and looked for ways to distract me from the pain.

When tears filled my eyes, Dad would say, "You're going to be just fine. Be strong."

I tried really hard to be strong and please my parents, but I wasn't sure how. The casts stayed on for weeks and weeks. When I got home, my sisters tried to entertain me, but I was often left by the window, watching them play outside. In the fall, me and my wheelchair were hauled back to the place for special kids.

Only I didn't feel special.

In time I got out of the wheelchair and onto crutches. But even after the ordeal was over, I could not walk correctly. My surgeon shook his head and said, "We need to try this again. I wish I understood exactly what the trouble is."

I was terrified. Another surgery. More pain. More handicapped school. More watching from the window. *What is wrong with me? Why can't I be like the other kids?*

～

"There's an Oral Roberts tent meeting in the San Fernando Valley next week," Mom said to Dad as they sat at dinner that evening. "Maybe we could take Valerie there and see if God will heal her."

"Worth a try," Dad said, chewing his chicken. "Worth a try."

On the night of the revival, Mom helped me put on my best dress. As we piled into the car, my parents seemed hopeful. I had only a vague understanding of what to expect, but I knew Oral Roberts might put his hands on me. That's what he did: he touched people and prayed. If I got touched, Jesus would heal my feet, and I would be like the other kids. I might as well have been going to Disneyland, I was so excited!

When we arrived, cars lined the parking lot. I couldn't believe how many sick people there were. Inside the tent, the press of the crowd gave me claustrophobia. I couldn't see over all the bodies as I maneuvered my tiny, crooked feet in the sawdust.

Anticipation was in the air—everyone waiting to be amazed. My father squeezed our family onto a bench as a tall, dark-haired man appeared onstage. An organ began blasting a hymn, and the massive crowd rose to its feet.

"God is here to heal!" cried Oral Roberts. "Come forward and receive!"

Quickly, a queue formed and Dad led me to our place in line. A man taking notes asked Dad what was wrong with me.

"She has trouble with her feet," he replied. "She's had an operation and needs another one."

The man wrote something down and went on to the next person.

Wide-eyed, I watched as Oral Roberts sat on a folding chair. A man behind him held a microphone to the preacher's face as he laid his hands on people, one by one.

"Little Jimmy, what's wrong with you?" the preacher asked a child who'd been placed in his lap.

Before the boy could answer, an announcer read what the man in front of the line had written down. "Pastor Roberts, Jimmy had polio when he was three, and now he can't move his right leg very well."

The preacher grabbed the boy's crippled leg and cried out to Jesus. "Heal this leg, in Your mighty name, dear Jesus!" Squinting his eyes shut, Oral Roberts pleaded fervently with God. After a moment of heart-stopping silence he opened his eyes and manipulated the boy's leg to see whether the stiffness had gone.

Hallelujah! It had!

"Now Jimmy," said Oral Roberts, "walk around here. Show everybody what Jesus has done for you."

The boy walked across the stage, demonstrating his complete healing. His mother cried joyful tears.

"Can you run for us, Jimmy?" Oral Roberts seemed to really enjoy the boy's healing.

Jimmy ran fast, up and down the aisles. And my hopeful heart soared.

People said their cancers were healed. Arthritis was vanquished. Various undefined illnesses were miraculously cured. One by one it looked like the whole tent was made well. Then, finally, my father stood me before the miracle-worker.

"What is wrong with this little girl?" he asked, his microphone feeding back.

"She has problems with her feet. Has already had one surgery and needs another," boomed the announcer.

I stood very still as Oral Roberts put his massive hands on my fragile feet. I held my breath as he cried out to God. "Jesus, heal this child's feet! Heal her now, in Your mighty name."

I waited. *Maybe my feet will tingle.*

"Can you stand up and move your feet for us, young lady?" asked the preacher.

"Yes, sir," I said, knowing they were going to be fine now.

But they weren't. I watched bewildered as everyone seemed to be healed but me. Ahead of me and behind me people rejoiced to see or hear again. Had I alone been passed over by God and left to suffer another surgery? Perhaps I wasn't sweet enough for God to care about. I felt embarrassed—ashamed, really—as my father and I returned to the bench where my disappointed mother waited.

~

Nobody understood what God was doing, especially not me. But life went on: Another surgery. More pain. Wheelchair. Crutches. St. Lawrence School for the Handicapped. By then, disease and surgeries seemed to define me. I was the handicapped child of Dean and Frances, Cheryl and Stephanie's weird sister.

Ironically, church was where I found my place. Mom decided I could sing. She made me practice hymns for solos in church. Not long after the second unsuccessful surgery, my father carried me to the platform and parked me in a chair, casts and all. The pianist began playing "Born to Serve the Lord." When she nodded her cue, I belted out the words: "My feet were made to walk in His footsteps. My body is the temple of the Lord."[1]

It was such a crowd-pleaser that I was asked to sing for the weekly radio program at the famed Angeles Temple in L.A. I sang, "I will always walk beside Him, for I was born to serve the Lord."[2]

It seemed the whole world listened. Two missionaries returning from a reservation in Arizona caught the broadcast while driving. They were so blessed by the child singing her heart out that they stopped by with a gift—a beaded necklace with a native girl dangling from the chain.

The song became a part of me. "My feet were made to walk in His footsteps…." The paradox was obvious. Often I changed the words and sang to myself: "My feet were made to have operations…"—several more operations, as it turned out. I was Valerie, the good little soldier, going into battle again. Each time, the elders prayed. Each time, healing seemed denied. And the seed of shame sprouted, wrapping my heart in its branches.

Cheryl

After the pastor's potluck, my mind drifted back to us three sisters growing up. Too quickly, the children who sang at church and played King on the Mountain became jaded. During our childhood, our family imploded. Our painful ordeal continued into our young adult lives. Mom and Dad were having trouble.

I noticed it first—a shifting in their relationship that made me uneasy.

By this time Valerie was in another handicapped school in Simi Valley. Our parents tried to get her into public school, but she had fallen behind academically. Becoming the class clown was Valerie's way out of the embarrassment. Her self-deprecating jokes and sarcastic touch won her lots of friends and gave her an edge.

One day we came home from school to find that Dad had moved out. "Our marriage is over," our mother said, matter-of-factly. "Dad won't be coming home."

What? Mom and Dad don't love each other anymore? It made no sense to me.

"Why can't you and Dad work things out, Mom?" I asked, trying to understand how this happened to a Christian family.

"It's too late for us." Mom said flatly.

"But, Mom, aren't Christians supposed to pray about things? I mean, haven't you always told us God answers prayer?"

Confusion, doubt, and anger rocked my soul. *What if none of it is true? What if all those songs we sing in church aren't real?*

"Well, maybe He does answer prayer," Mom offered, "but He didn't save us."

"Did you and Dad even pray?" A sense of desperation choked me and I sobbed. In my head played the words they always sang at church: "Prayer is the key to heaven, but faith unlocks the door."[3]

Then we should pray! It's that simple.

There was no more explanation from my mother. I was left to wonder and try to understand things on my own. There was no closure for her oldest child.

I walked out of the house and down the street. Unanswered questions submerged me in grief. *Where are You, God?* It was a question I would ask over and over again for the next tumultuous years of my young life.

Life became a shipwreck, and I wrestled with the sense that God had abandoned us. So I ran away from Him. No one seemed to notice, not even Mom. One day while watching her primp for a date, I asked, "What happened, Mom? How come you go out all the time now?"

There had to be a reason. I knew Mom loved us. She was a good woman who seemed to take a wrong turn. Now my question had to be answered, and it would be hard to do. Mom swiped her lipstick across her top lip, trying to talk at the same time.

"Your father was never home," she said.

"He worked all the time, Mom." *What does that excuse even mean?*

"You'll understand when you're older," she said, recapping the lipstick and fluffing her hair. "I got lonely." She turned from the mirror and looked at me. "I guess it all just took its toll."

She was right. I wasn't old enough to understand. But at least she answered me. At least she let me see the resignation in her eyes.

"I'll see you and your sisters later." And she was out of the house.

The door had barely shut before I sneaked out for the night. The crowd I'd found was rough, into drugs and rowdy parties. My stomping away from faith needed medication to dull the ache. Maybe God cared even if my parents didn't. Maybe He would notice how much I hurt. Even stop me, perhaps.

Always the question rose up inside me: *How could You let this happen to our family?*

~

"I'm going to Grandma's," said Valerie when I asked why she was packing her overnight bag. "I like it better over there."

Mom and I were hard to watch, even partying together at times. So I tossed out a rhetorical question. "How come?"

Valerie answered me. "I can't deal with you and Mom going out all the time. It's not right. I like it better at Grandma's."

Valerie's departures became a weekend habit. So did drugs, bars, and iffy relationships for my mom and me. Mother and daughter had plunged off the deep end together with no bottom in sight.

"Why doesn't Dad come around anymore?" Valerie wanted to know.

"He's got his own life," Mom said, sipping reheated coffee one afternoon.

"He used to try to make things better," Valerie offered. "Then I think he quit."

The family had gone to pot. Whatever used to hold us together was now unglued.

"I wish things were the way they used to be," Valerie said, looking at the floor as Mom stared out the window.

"Sorry, Valerie." What else could Mom say?

$\sim$

As the months wore on, a cycle of disrespect got out of hand. The more Mom tried to make rules for me, the more I broke them. Valerie, on the other hand, was middle-child conscientious, always wanting to obey and please our mother. One night, I talked Valerie into attending a party with me. She understood our curfew to be midnight and started bugging me when it was time to leave.

"Nah…" I said, waving at my little sister with the back of my hand.

"Come on, Cheryl," said Valerie, tugging my arm. "Mom said we've got to be home by midnight!"

We missed curfew by thirty minutes, yet Mom asked, "What're you two doing here so early?"

Valerie was confused. "You said to be home by midnight."

"Oh…" said Mom. "Okay." She thought a moment, and added. "Valerie, you need to go with Cheryl all the time. I know you'll get her home."

That didn't last long. Valerie began drinking for courage. Most of the parties were out in the sticks among people she didn't even know. I would disappear for hours saying, "Oh, I'll be right back!"

My shy sister would sometimes go and sit in the car. After a while, it was easier to just join the party. Have a few drinks. Talk with drunk people she didn't know. Try to engage with them in order to feel like part of the crowd. But her conscience was pricked. She hated doing wrong and feared the consequences. Her teenage heart was attached to Jesus in a way mine no longer was.

I was not ready for sleep when we came home at night. Instead, I tried to walk off my heartache in the damp overnight air. The addictions that eased my pain only masked the real issue. *Where are You, God? Why did You leave us like this? I pounded the pavement with my prayers, accusations, and pleas. We used to be a family, God!*

Tears streaked my cheeks as I wiped my nose with my sleeve. *Is He even listening?* How I missed believing that He was. How homesick I was for the way life used to be. *Talk to me, Jesus! Tell me why!* Angry and craving His response, I wanted to have it out with God like Job did. I wanted answers to satisfy the void. Then I would drag myself home to bed.

∼

Immersed in her own emotions, Mom didn't see school as a priority for her oldest daughter. There were enough challenges without worrying about whether or not I graduated. As early as the eighth grade, I missed more than a month of school. After two weeks home with tonsillitis, it was time to return to classes. But Mom said, "Let's redecorate the house instead."

For two weeks we wallpapered and painted the place. It sounded like more fun than English and math. But one afternoon during my third week off, the phone rang.

"Hey, Cheryl," said one of my friends. "Are you ever coming back to school?"

"I guess so," I replied.

I hadn't really thought about it. With no money in the house, I had given up on participating in school activities. Between our finances and my absenteeism, my aspirations as a cheerleader were dashed. There would be no prom dates. No pretty dresses.

School no longer seemed important.

Meanwhile, we rarely saw Dad except on weekends. Every other week, we girls went to his girlfriend's house and tried to act like it was normal. I could not have articulated it then, but I'm sure this fed my rebellion. My heart knew the arrangement was wrong. But I was just a kid; I didn't know what to do except kick against the pain.

Eventually, I became too much for my parents to handle—always in trouble and acting out. My mother sent me to Cottonwood, Arizona, to stay with a Christian friend of hers. But mothering from a substitute didn't really help me. I wanted my own mom to get a grip. *I wanted her back the way she used to be.*

Finally, Mom came to the end of herself. Her life caved in and she looked up. Dad still loved her. God still loved both of them. Divorce had taught them a lot. This time they were really committed. They understood what it meant to be away from each other and from God. So they remarried.

But smoothing out the rocky road behind us was not easy. When I returned from Arizona, I quit school, took a factory job, and moved in with my boyfriend. I couldn't cope at home anymore. A few months later, I told my dad I was getting married. His only response was: "You know you can't wear white."

Yeah. I knew. The dress was ivory. As I walked down the aisle at Panorama Full Gospel Church, I carried a bouquet of plastic flowers dressed with sprigs of live baby's breath. I said, "I do"— but not to a fairy-tale prince.

Moving On

Valerie

Dad's job transferred him, so he and Mom started over in Flagstaff, Arizona. They left their house in California for Cheryl and me to live in, along with Cheryl's daughter, Shannon.

For obvious reasons, my sister's marriage lasted less than eighteen months. But in its wake, Cheryl had grown up. She quit her rough life and settled into motherhood. Meanwhile, I, too, dropped out of high school and bought a used car from my Uncle Lance.

There was one problem: I was underage and had no license or insurance. Lance's wife, Violeta, was Mom's sister. I let it slip that I was driving all over California. Circumstances soon prohibited me from staying in the state, and I ended up in Flagstaff, the one-horse town where nothing ever happened. There I lost my car and my independence. But I discovered that my parents cared about what I was doing.

In Flagstaff I could not escape my sister Stephanie's social life, which involved making friends via CB radio. Stephanie's handle was Silver Streak, because she had a mouthful of braces. She and I lived with Mom and Dad at the Kit Carson RV Park, which attracted lodgers and travelers. Many of our neighbors worked with Dad as Greyhound drivers. Between trips they rested up, telling stories and drinking in their RVs. Like an extended family, they all knew each other's business.

One afternoon, Stephanie dropped by with Brian, a tall, blond guy she met talking over the CB. A neighbor was in his driveway when they walked up. Brian had an hour to kill, so he pulled up a seat. Turns out he wasn't really interested in sixteen-year-old Silver Streak. But when I walked by with my Aunt Julie (who was young enough to be my friend), Brian couldn't take his eyes off me.

I had someone else on my mind, however, and Brian wasn't my type. All that changed one Saturday afternoon when Julie and I went cruising down Route 66. We had the radio blaring and the windows open when Brian pulled beside us at a stoplight.

"Hey, where you ladies goin'?" he asked as he leaned out the window, cocking his head and trying to look less nervous than he was.

"El Rancho grocery store," I said, with my hand draped over the steering wheel.

"I'll follow you there."

When we pulled up to the grocery store parking lot, Brian was right behind us. On weekends local hot-rodders parked at El Rancho to talk cars and meet girls. It was Flagstaff's weekend hot spot.

"You're Valerie, Stephanie's sister, right?" asked Brian when we stepped out of the car. "I'm Brian, remember?"

"Yes. At Kit Carson's the other afternoon." I was trying to be coy.

Looking at Julie, he asked, "Who's this?" Brian had forgotten that they'd already met, so I introduced them.

"Can I take you two out for a drink?" he asked, scratching his head nervously.

We answered in unison. "Sure. Why not?"

Brian and I soon married in California. He was unfaithful to me before the honeymoon should have been over. The marriage lasted six months. He didn't want me anymore, and filed for divorce. I was used. Discarded. The handicapped kid and weird sister of Cheryl and Stephanie. And now the abandoned wife of Brian, the cheater.

Cheryl

When Brian married Valerie, his friend Dave Schuelke attended the wedding. Brian and Dave had both grown up in Wisconsin.

"Cheryl, you've got to meet Dave," Valerie said. "He's really cute, and a really nice guy!"

After the wedding Dave returned to Flagstaff, where I moved after leaving my husband for good. With my divorce almost final, I had no use for another man. At first, Dave wasn't too interested, either. But he had promised to take care of Brian's house while he and Valerie honeymooned.

One afternoon Mom called to check on Brian's dogs and ended up chatting with Dave. "Why don't you take my daughter Cheryl out?" she asked. "She lives here now and needs some friends."

There was more on Mom's mind than that. But Dave was a nice guy and soon after that, he took me to one of the nicest restaurants in Flagstaff. I'd never really been on a dress-up date at a really nice place. Over steak and lobster, we discovered each other. For three weeks we were inseparable.

Then Dave dropped the bombshell that scared me to death. "I love you."

Whoa! I was not yet divorced and still had a twinge of hope for my marriage. I balked and wouldn't see Dave again.

After several weeks, he said, "I can't take this, Cheryl. I'm moving back to Wisconsin. I need to try and get over you."

And he did. I missed the guy more than I expected. He flew to Arizona a couple of times and wired me flowers. He won my heart, came back to Flagstaff, and married me.

Dave is the love of my life.

Notes

1. Bud Chambers, "Born to Serve the Lord," Peermusic, 1959.
2. Ibid.
3. Samuel T. Scott, Robert L. Sands, "Faith Unlocks the Door (Prayer Is the Key to Heaven)," Duchess Music Corporation, 1945, renewed rights administered by MCA Music Publications (a division of MCA, Inc.).

3

STEPS TOWARD HEAVEN (VALERIE)

For three years after my divorce, I lived with my parents. I took a job at a Circle K and settled into life. Then Gentry, a young trucker, moved in next door. Dad thought he was a nice guy. I didn't meet him until UPS left a package for him on our doorstep.

A couple of nights later, Gentry walked into Circle K.

"Hey, I think I have something for you," I said, smiling at him.

He looked surprised. "You do?"

"Yeah. A package from UPS." I laughed.

"Oh, that." Gentry seemed deflated.

He came to pick up the package when he knew I'd be home. We immediately hit it off and began spending time together, going out and talking on the phone. We had what I thought was a fun relationship, despite his confusing behavior.

Gentry had a short fuse, and I couldn't seem to stay on his right side. It should have been a red flag, but I missed it. Five months later, I married him, more in love with the idea of love than anything else. My high hopes were short-lived. In the end, I felt discounted and mistreated.

Shame kept me from telling anyone that my second marriage was on the rocks. On some level, I thought I deserved it. Dad found out, though. He came to the house one afternoon and took my young husband aside.

"I'm going to give you the benefit of the doubt, young man," Dad said with his face up against Gentry's. "But if I ever hear that you are mistreating my daughter, I'll come over here and set things right!"

Gentry withered. Dad squared his shoulders and walked out. The message had been received. Things changed, but not really. The marriage barely held through the birth of our daughter, Elissa. With another failed marriage in under two years, my *less than* label reappeared. I was incapable of relationship and flawed in some way that I could not define.

Another Try

There was a convenience store in the old neighborhood where Brian and I had lived. A friend of mine managed the store and promised to give me some boxes I needed for packing. One Wednesday evening, Mom went there with me. She was cooing over Elissa when Brian came in.

My heartbeat sped up, and I got mad at myself. *Why should I care?*

Brian approached hesitantly and said, "Hi." He looked disheveled and surprised to see me.

I just nodded. Something seemed stuck in my throat, as if there was so much to say that I couldn't respond at all.

Brian looked at his feet. "I heard..." He stopped and cleared his throat. "Well, someone said you and Gentry broke up." He looked up warily. "That true?"

"Yeah," I offered. I would rather have told anyone but Brian that another marriage failed.

When Mom walked over with Elissa, the conversation detoured. "Oh, there's your baby," said Brian as he reached for Elissa's hand. "She's cute."

Brian talked briefly with Mom, but seemed unable to concentrate and more interested in my chat with the manager. He did tell me later that, on the way out the door, he prayed: "Lord, You think I can have another chance with her?"

It took a few days before Brian summoned the courage to call me. "Can I talk to you a minute? Please," he said and held his breath.

"About what?" I asked, trying to conceal my hopefulness.

"Maybe seeing you?" There it was. He held his breath again.

"What?" I was stunned and a little put off.

"Seeing you—can I see you again?"

"You mean go out?"

"Yeah. Something like that."

The silence was loaded, each of us trying to find what to say next.

Finally, I spoke. "My car needs a tune-up."

"Could I do that?" Brian asked, almost falling over himself. "Would you let me tune up your car? I could do that. I could do it Saturday."

"Okay. Fine." *What could that hurt? It'll save me money.* "Elissa and I will be there around ten in the morning."

"Good."

I could tell Brian was trying to think of something to say. I made him squirm just a little. "Is that all you wanted?"

"Uh…I guess so." He seemed to hate the idea of hanging up.

I helped end the call. "Well, see you Saturday."

~

Cheryl couldn't believe the news. "You said *what?*"

"He could tune up my car. It needs a tune-up, Cheryl."

"There are plenty of mechanics in Flagstaff, Valerie! My gosh! The man broke your heart in pieces. What are you thinking?"

"That my car needs a tune-up." I was hedging. What I wanted was to see whether Brian had really changed.

On Saturday, I arrived with Elissa in tow. When Brian finished the tune-up he asked, "Do you think you might have dinner with me sometime?"

I felt conflicted and couldn't answer him. Everything I once found attractive about Brian was still there.

Would I be a fool to say yes?

"I'd like to take you out," Brian tried once more. "Would you go out with me again?"

"I guess so," I answered. "Yeah. Why not?"

On Monday night, Elissa fussed on the way to meet Brian. I wondered how he would handle a cranky baby and an ex-wife. Elissa seemed to like him, which made me more comfortable with him, too. It was a little hard to talk over her whining, but Brian gave it a shot.

He reached for my hand and said, "You know, Valerie, I should never have let you go." He cleared his throat, betraying his nervousness. "I'll even go to church with you."

He was fishing for anything that would commend him to me again.

"That's good," I said. Then, uncomfortable with the sentimentality, I withdrew my hand and reached for Elissa.

"No, really, Valerie." Brian made me look into his eyes. "I told God I would do anything if He would give me a second chance with you."

I had nothing to say. I still loved him, but was unsure I could trust him.

"I'm different, Valerie," he persisted. "Please let me prove it to you."

My heart and my head argued all the way home. I knew I still cared for Brian, but Cheryl was livid. "Are you crazy, Valerie?" She almost screamed it. "You would let him hurt you again?"

"I guess the answer is yes, Cheryl. I still love him."

Six months later I remarried my first love in a Las Vegas chapel. There was no fanfare. Life simply moved on. But the old ruts showed up, along with some new ones. Even the birth of Ashley could not help our failing second marriage. Brian worked seven days a week from early morning to late at night. As soon as he walked into the house he relaxed with his new mistress—drink.

For years, I asked him to spend time with me and the girls.

"I like things just the way they are," he'd say.

Back in the Fold

I was wiping down the kitchen counters when the back door opened. "Hi, Mom," I said as she entered with a book in her hand.

"I was out this morning and thought I'd come by," she said, sliding the book onto the counter. "How are you this morning?"

It was a hard question to answer. There were days when life seemed a little less hopeless. This was one of those days. "Fine, Mom."

She was back in church, and I was glad for her. Carrying her coffee cup to the table, she broached the topic. "Have you found a church yet?"

"No." I poured myself a cup and sat down. "I've gone to a couple, but there's nothing out there that I like. No place that I feel I belong."

"Well, I brought that book for you. You should read it."

I glanced over, with no intention of reading anything religious. "Okay, Mom. Thanks," End of conversation.

Six months later life had hit bottom again. I wandered into the kitchen and scooped up the book. I read the first few pages and lost myself in the message. The author said there should be power in the Christian life. He hinted at something more…something deeper. For the first time in years, I wanted to know what that *something* was.

Maybe I should go back to church.

Finding a church wasn't easy. I'd taken Elissa and Ashley to services at several local congregations, but always left feeling like something was lacking. Canyon Chapel Church changed that. I'd visited on Wednesdays for special speakers, so I assumed they had regular midweek services. The pastor's wife, Jane Lankhorst, met my friend Mary and me at the door. "We don't have a Wednesday night service. We're only here to meet the youth group. They're coming back from a mission trip."

As we turned to leave, Jane said, "I hope you'll come back. We have services on Sundays, and other things happening all through the week."

I saw something in Jane's eyes. Something drew me to the place. Finally! A church where I belonged. A place where I could heal and receive a revelation of my worth.

A Word for the Bride

I got very involved at the church, but it was in prayer that I felt a special sense of purpose. Soon after joining the prayer group, I was speaking with a Christian couple, Mitchell and Rhonda, whom I'd known for several months. I was telling them how finding Canyon Chapel was like finding home.

They listened politely and asked some questions. Then something unexpected happened. I saw a vision of a bride standing at the back of a church, ready to walk down the aisle. The experience distracted me. Mitchell was speaking, but I politely interrupted him.

"Mitchell, I see the Lord standing with His Bride, about to walk down the aisle. There seems to be some hesitation on her part, so Jesus asks her, 'Are you going to marry Me?' The Bride's eyes are glazed over. She seems unable to answer His question. Her dress is filthy and ragged, with strings hanging loose where beads once were. And other beads are hanging by a thread."

In that moment I knew I was to address Mitchell's wife. It took all my courage to turn to her and say, "Rhonda, you are one of those beads hanging by a thread. God knows that."

She began to cry. When she composed herself, she thanked me for saying what I did. Mitchell might have said something, too, but it escaped me. As I walked away, I prayed that I had done the right thing.

Not long afterward, Rhonda left Mitchell and Jesus. Another bead dropped from the garment of His Bride, the Church. Later on, I wondered about the whole experience.

"You have a prophetic gift," Jane kept saying.

"Why do you say that? I don't tell the future."

"That's not necessarily what it means to be prophetic," Jane said as she put her arm on my shoulder. "It means you see things in another dimension. You can interpret our times." She smiled. "So can I."

"Other people think that's weird, Jane."

"I know. But you and I are in good company with the apostle Paul and John the revelator. The prophetic is real even though it makes people uncomfortable. Sometimes it makes *us* feel uncomfortable."

Jane's affirmation refreshed me. The picture of Jesus and His Bride kept coming back to me in the Thursday prayer group. The Bride is the Church, redeemed and dressed in white. Jesus said in the book of Matthew that she must make herself ready for His coming.[1] Even though the wait is long, the Bride must not become complacent or drowsy.

I knew that kind of readiness demanded a fervency that I and other Christians had been missing. It was hard to shake the awful thought of Jesus returning to find His Church roused from sleep with matted hair and a crumpled dress.

"How do we pray for Christians to get ready?" I asked in a Thursday morning meeting late in 1999. "I keep seeing the Bride at the doorway with her glazed-over expression and dirty gown. If that's what the Church looks like to Jesus, what will we do?"

"Probably start with ourselves," said Cheryl, who joined the church about the time I did. "Pray for our own lives to be cleaned up. Pray for the Church to look alive and ready and dressed for Him."

"Lord, give us a vision of the Bride," I prayed as the worship cassette ended and the ladies were quiet. "What does she look like to You?"

"And how do we become beautiful again?" added Cheryl.

The answer to our prayer was only weeks away.

The Question

It first came like a faraway echo. I thought I heard it wrong, so I dismissed it. It seemed crazy, and my answer would most certainly be "No." Valerie Paters didn't take life seriously, much less death. My job was to liven up the party. Thinking too deeply about things only confused me. So the question—"Valerie, will you die for Me?"—was too ominous to consider.

The first time I heard it, I was sitting in the large sanctuary at Canyon Chapel. I'd already dropped off Ashley at school and driven to church on my favorite day—Thursday, when our prayer group met.

Cheryl sat quietly as a worship tape played. Eleven people had gathered to pray, but all were silent. Cheryl broke the silence. "I feel the Lord wants to speak to us about counting the cost of being Christians. He's been asking me whether I'm willing to understand more deeply what He endured on the cross for us."

Several of the intercessors agreed that God was telling them the same thing. Cheryl looked earnestly at the group. "I don't think we know how much He loves us. We've heard it. Our minds try to comprehend it, but we don't really know it with our hearts."

"Because sometimes life makes us think otherwise," I offered.

There was assent from the group that my statement was true, but no one asked what caused me to doubt the depth of God's love.

"If we really understood how much Christ loves us, wouldn't that change the way we live?" asked another woman. "Wouldn't we be more secure? Maybe even fearless?"

The question hung in the air. Then Cheryl began to pray. "Lord, please help us to understand how much You care for us. Teach us to count the cost and go all the way with You."

Prayer continued as some intercessors fell prostrate before God. Long minutes of silence were interrupted by soft weeping and crying out to Him. These times of intercession made me more and more uncomfortable. *What price?* I didn't know whether I was ready to go all the way with God. The idea stirred up feelings of emptiness, self-hatred, and anger. I'd spent my adult life denying the feelings, yet there they were. Random memories and hidden thoughts confused me, like puzzle pieces without a picture to explain what the thing was supposed to look like.

"Lord," I whispered, "I don't know what You want from me."

"Pray what you mean," seemed to be His answer.

This was not a joke. God was excavating my heart and I could not ignore it. My old façade could not conceal the river raging inside me. Fear of it had kept me laughing and denying the pain for too long. Now it was time to be real and pray what I meant. So I did: "I don't know what You see when You look at me, but I'm pretty sure it's ugly. You do things for others that You refuse to do for me."

There. I'd said it, but my honesty scared me to death. *Who am I to tell God I'm mad at Him? I am nothing. I have always been nothing.*

Then I heard it—the first whisper of God's question: "Valerie, will you die for Me?"

My perception seemed shaky. *That probably wasn't the voice of God.* So I dismissed it for the moment.

But over the coming weeks, the question did not relent. Whether in the tax office or at home…whether driving or meeting with the prayer group, it remained.

No. No. No! I don't even know what that means. Will I die for You?

No. I don't think so.

Facing the Feelings

Once God began digging deep in me, I wasn't myself anymore. Trying hard to mean every word I said to Him, I curbed the way I prayed. "Paying the price…counting the cost…going all the way"—I was not really feeling any of it. Every time Thursday intercession reached that place, I shut down inside. I could not even join the others for lunch.

Full of anger, I asked Him: "Where in the world were You when I needed You?" How could I go all the way with God if I didn't feel safe with Him? I couldn't. I went home on Thursdays, and threw myself on the living room floor. *God, I don't know what to do with all that I'm seeing in me. I'm so angry! I didn't know it before, but I know it now.*

Over and over, God reminded me that only He could take my anger. "Empty your heart," He said. "Let Me heal it."

I questioned the feelings I could no longer deny. *Should I be feeling these things, much less verbalizing them to God?* The psalms assured me that David hadn't spared the Lord his raw feelings. They were all out there, and they weren't pretty.

Feeling what I had never before allowed myself to feel, I remembered the accusation: "Your sister's retarded!" How many times had I heard it? Cheryl and one of her friends even beat up a girl who made fun of me. But that didn't make me normal. And what about the divorce and the chaos it caused? And all those prayer meetings and surgeries?

No wonder I hated myself. God had been on the sidelines the whole time, yet He never intervened. *Why, God? You could've changed everything. But You didn't!*

The times in prayer were cleansing, but with so much buried in my heart, the process could take forever! Ever since my formative years I had been out of control, unprotected, and miserable. No boundaries. No accountability. No nothing.

"I hate You, God!"

There. It was ugly, but it was honest. I lay on the floor and waited, then yelled, "You were not there!"

With each confrontation, more debris came loose and a new peace followed. The God who seemed so distant had heard me. He was there, listening, not wanting me to feel desolate any longer.

I drank in His presence and allowed Him to love me.

Surrender

The lives of the martyrs began to intrigue me, so I read about them extensively. Still, I pushed *my* dying for Him to the back burner. Maybe I could say yes once I understood why the martyrs did. But now, the thought scared me. Was He going to kill me? Take my kids? How could any of that be His plan?

I wondered whether Jesus had asked His friend Lazarus to die for Him. Maybe Lazarus left this world knowing he would come back in four days. God had obviously allowed his death in order to amaze the world. That meant Jesus was not safe—not like I thought of safety. He had not kept Lazarus or his sisters from suffering. After the man died, his sisters asked Jesus my question: "Where were You?"

If Jesus is asking me to die for Him, there must be a reason, one I couldn't possibly guess.

In late 1999, as I lay once again on my living room floor, I said, "Okay, God. I'm scared," I searched for the courage to answer His question, but only repeated myself. "I know You want everything. But, I'm so scared."

Finally, the question weighed so heavily I knew I could not go on without answering it. "Okay. I'll die for You…but, I'm scared, God. Really scared."

It was done.

Note

1. See Matthew 24:44.

4

From One Life to the Next

Signs, Semis, and a Shift

Cheryl

In January 2000 I had a disturbing dream: I drove past an accident scene as traffic slowed to a crawl. Fear gripped me. My heart pounded. Several semis had crashed into each other…fatally. The cabs had folded into one another like accordions. Their loads had overturned and spilled onto the slick pavement.

In slow motion, I absorbed the carnage into some deeper place in my subconscious. Instead of waking with a start, I seemed to drive out of the dream and back into the safety of my bed. Yet I remained troubled by what I had seen.

"Jesus, please protect us," I prayed in the darkness. "Please keep us all safe from such a thing as this."

I slept again, but fitfully. All day the nightmare replayed in my mind. Each time, my heart raced, and I prayed. Finally, it lifted.

Valerie

On March 20, 2000, I climbed into my silver Jeep Cherokee and threw my purse into the back seat. The heavy snowfall had tapered off by the time I picked up Ashley from school. But as she sang along with the car stereo, snow descended suddenly.

Visibility was poor as I slowed down. A semi had already pulled onto the right shoulder. I moved close to it, in the right-hand lane, and stopped the car.

"We should be okay right here," I said as the car idled.

In Flagstaff, it wasn't unusual to wait out a sudden change in weather. Wrecks on I-40 were common. I knew we would be there for a while, but I had no idea what would happen behind us.

Moments after pulling over, I looked in the rearview mirror. A big rig was careening toward us. The driver had braked too late. The unstoppable machine was about to devour Ashley and me. "Jesus! Jesus! Jesus!" was all I had time to say.

The enormous truck slammed into the back of our car, crushing the back seat into the front. One of our passenger doors flew off. Ashley was ejected from her seatbelt, and landed on the pavement. Squealing tires and crunching metal were the only sounds as the Jeep's front end lunged under the parked semi.

In a split second, another big rig flew into the jackknifed truck. Both slammed the Jeep once again. The impact flung my body sideways into the seat Ashley had just vacated. Now the Jeep was completely under the parked truck. I was trapped, barely alive and unaware that Ashley lay unconscious on the icy ground.

I opened my eyes, but they wouldn't focus. In front of me was what I thought to be the glove compartment. My legs were wedged in where the steering wheel used to be. The passenger seat cradled my head. A seatbelt seemed to be cutting me in two. I realized all of this in a flash of consciousness before the unbearable pain began.

The space was filled with primal moaning. It was mine, but I heard it as though I were out of my body and hearing someone else. The smell of gasoline melded with the sounds of shouts and sirens. With no breath to muster, I lost the will to cry out.

Then I passed through a door to a large room. It was tranquil, with brilliant white walls and high ceilings.

Where am I?

Slowly I moved toward a golden, velvety, circular sofa in the center of the room. It seemed too smooth and insubstantial to hold my weight.

What am I doing here?

The answer didn't matter. I was in the most perfectly peaceful place.

"Ma'am! Ma'am!" Tearing into my peace was a loud voice. "Ma'am! Ma'am, can you hear me?"

I could, but barely.

"Ma'am, I'm Captain Bob Hiser of the Fire Department. You've been in an accident. You're going to be okay. You hear? We're going to get you out of there! Just stay with me, okay? Hang on!"

I could not see the captain's face as he lay on his stomach amid tire tread and metal. Too short of breath to speak, I listened as he inched away, scraping the wet pavement. The sound made me dizzy. The toxic air was nauseating. It reeked of exhaust and burnt rubber.

"How are we going to get her out of there?" The firefighter's earlier encouragement had collided with the impossibility of the situation.

A claustrophobic panic seized me. *I have to get out of here!* Disoriented, I fought the ruins that entrapped me, but my body seemed unable to obey my commands. There was no pushing or pulling. No kicking or stretching. I was bound. Whatever movement I mustered brought searing pain.

"Jesus, help me," I uttered as life drained from my body. I knew that I was dying. "Jesus, help me, *please.*"

What I needed was to get still, just like after my childhood surgeries. All those months stuck in bed with my legs elevated—movement was excruciating. So I reminded myself: *Calm down. Wait. I did it then. I can do it now.*

Breathing was exhausting. Closing my eyes was much easier. Again, I rested on the golden sofa and inhaled the peace. I didn't wonder again about where I was; I only marveled at the pristine loveliness of the place.

"Ma'am!" A young man inched closer. "I'm James Robinson, a paramedic. I'm trying to get to you. So stay with me, ma'am. Hang on!"

Suspended between heaven and Earth, my mind was jumbled. I had to force myself to listen to James.

"Work with me, ma'am!" He sensed that he was losing me.

I tried to do what he said. But I longed for the golden sofa, where I was happy and whole. *I think that's me on the couch, but how can I watch her and be her at the same time? How can I see what she's thinking unless she's me?* The delicious thought came that at any moment a door would open and I would be invited through it.

The Rescue

Dave Dobbs got the call—a massive wreck on I-40. Too many emergency vehicles were coming from the east. Traffic was backed up for more than a mile behind the twisted cars and trucks.

"Take your engine around from the west. Maybe you can get through faster," the dispatcher said before hanging up.

Dave was uneasy about his orders. *What if the cars that got through before the pileup come at me in the lanes going east?* Sirens blaring and lights flashing, Dave drove his ladder truck cautiously. His was the first one on the scene. He found several semis crushed together and people milling around in freezing temperatures.

He tried to take it all in. It was a mess. "We're going to need all the trucks we can get," Dave told the dispatcher. Then he stepped down from his.

I'm going to show you some things. Dave shivered. He knew God was speaking.

After walking a few feet, he kicked something. It was a cassette. His stomach churned. What he'd always feared might be happening. Someone he knew might be in this accident. He picked up the tape. The label said *Canyon Chapel.* It was a teaching tape from his church.

Oh, God.

"There's a car trapped under that semi!" Someone yelled at Dave.

"You sure?" He couldn't see how it was possible. At first he could not even see the car. But he saw a Jeep hood ornament on the pavement. The pinned-down car was silver.

A woman stood beside the wreckage, bending over as she shook in the cold. "I think somebody moved in there!"

No way. No one lived through this nightmare. Dave crouched down to look where the woman was pointing. Barely visible through the blown-out window was Valerie's black hair. Dave put two and two together. The Jeep. The teaching tape. The dark hair. *I know this woman from church. It's Cheryl's sister.*

"Look!" yelled the shivering woman again. "See? Her hand moved!"

Light glinted off a diamond from the bracelet Cheryl had given Valerie for her birthday.

"Look! She's moving!"

She was, but not much.

Dave's hands shook as he called his wife. "Hon, Cheryl's sister Valerie is in this accident on I-40. It doesn't look good." He took a deep breath. "Better call Cheryl. Tell her to get to the hospital. We're trying to figure out how to get her sister out from under a huge truck."

Meanwhile, Ashley lay in a triangle of pavement formed by the semi on the shoulder and the first truck that hit Valerie's Jeep. It was the only place on the scene that could have protected her from the impact of the second truck and subsequent wrecks. Unconscious and severely injured, Ashley was rushed to the first ambulance on the scene. No one knew who she was.

"Man, it's a miracle that kid survived!" Bob Hiser found Dave as he walked back from the emergency vehicle.

"Who was she?" Dave hadn't seen her before the ambulance left.

"Don't know, yet. But she should've been dead," said Bob. "You can't train for this," he continued, shaking his head. "This is the most difficult situation I've seen in my eighteen years! We've got to get that woman out from under that semi," he yelled back as he ran to radio for backup and the Jaws of Life.

~

Nine fire department units and twenty-one fire personnel responded to the enormous crash scene. Even off-duty firemen were called up. Valerie's car was one of sixteen vehicles involved. Eight other people also needed help, but over a dozen firefighters were focused on finding the best way to extract Valerie's car.

"We've got to lift this semi first!"

Dave noticed that a truck in the far left lane was leaking propane. "We have a major hazmat issue over here, guys!" he yelled. "Unless we get fans on it before we use the Jaws this whole scene could go up in a blaze of glory!"

Everything was taking time, something Valerie was short on. She was too still, not very responsive, and drifting in and out of consciousness. The medic wanted to check her pulse. He kept crawling beneath the truck but could not reach her.

The rear of the car was jammed accordion-style into the front seat. The driver's door was intact, but the passenger door was missing. James heard that there was a young girl in the car. Apparently the driver of the parked truck had noticed her. *If she's in the back seat, she's dead.*

An hour into the rescue, giant fans blew the propane away from Valerie's car. A hydraulic pump raised the rear end of the semi as firefighters stacked two-by-fours under the suspended wheels. James still couldn't reach the trapped woman, who was now quiet.

"She's wearing down!" shouted James. "We're running out of time!"

"Keep talking to her, son!" Captain Hiser answered as he shoved another piece of wood in place.

With the truck lifted and secured, James made it to the car. The wrist with the bracelet was the only accessible part of Valerie's body.

"She has a pulse!" he cried.

Until the giant pincers cut away the car's roof, the medic could not reach Valerie's face to administer oxygen. She needed oxygen; the dashboard on the passenger side was crushing her chest. Yet Dave marveled because, as tiny as it was, she was in the only space in which she could have survived.

As the Jaws of Life cut away metal, the dispatcher radioed Dave. "Who's missing a child?"

It must be Valerie's daughter. Thank God she wasn't in that back seat. Dave called his wife again. "Call Cheryl again. Tell her they already brought in Valerie's child. Cheryl needs to identify her in emergency."

Dave called the emergency room. "We're pretty sure the girl belongs to the lady trapped beneath a truck here on I-40. We'll get her mother there as soon as we can extricate her."

Dave overheard one of the firefighters as he walked back to the rescue operation. "It doesn't make sense that this door flew off or that the seatbelt disengaged. Both doors should've stayed in place the way this wreck happened."

They scratched their chins.

"Neither one of them would've made it if that had happened," Dave added. "They would've been decapitated. But the young lady was in that triangle over there."

They knew they'd seen something inexplicable. They had too many wrecks under their belts and had seen too few amazing outcomes to explain this.

"It's the miracle triangle," said Dave.

"It's off!" cried the firefighter who lifted the final section of roof from the Jeep, revealing Valerie's broken body.

"Get the seatbelt off her!" cried James as he took her pulse. A gurney appeared beside the medic. "She's still alive."

But Valerie's pulse was weak. James couldn't make her respond.

Piece by piece, the men carefully removed the wreckage that had entombed Valerie for more than two hours. Finally, she was freed, her broken body flopping like a rag doll. The firefighters and medic braced her neck and slid her onto the gurney. The rescue was over, and they hadn't lost her. Not yet.

Dave Dobbs took his first deep breath in hours, and tears fell to his cheeks. With Valerie and the metal that once covered her removed, he saw something on the floor of the car. It was a book by Myda Kelton—*Nothing Is Impossible With God.*

Only God could've saved those two. You are right, Lord. Today I have seen some things.

Front view of Jeep Cherokee

Driver's side of Valerie's car

Where Valerie was trapped (front passenger compartment)

Valerie and her friend, Captain/paramedic Dave Dobbs reunite (May 2014)

Valerie thanks paramedic James Robinson.

The Edge of Life and Death (Cheryl)

Nancy Dobbs called my friend Jan about the wreck. Jan then relayed the terrifying news. "Cheryl?"

Jan's call raised my suspicions. "Yes?"

My mind was racing. There was that vague memory of this having happened, in a dream, maybe.

"Nancy just got a call from Dave…"

I knew then that Valerie was in the accident. Dave was a firefighter and must have responded to the scene. I felt myself quake and shiver.

"Your sister was involved in a huge pileup near the Butler Avenue exit of I-40. They're trying to get her out of her car. When they do, she'll be transported to Flagstaff Medical Center. She's in very critical condition." Jan waited for a response then continued. "Cheryl, you might want to be there when the ambulance arrives."

Stunned, I put down the receiver. *What is happening, God? Is Valerie going to die? Is that what You want? How do You want me to pray?*

My questions were not rhetorical. I needed His answers *now*. So I listened.

"Pray that she will live and not die and declare the works of the Lord," was what I heard. *Psalms 118:17—that is what I will pray.*

In that moment I knew Valerie would make it. What I didn't know was how fierce the battle would be.

I changed into jeans and a sweater, and grabbed the phone. "Mom, what are you and Dad doing?"

"Bringing in some things from the car. Why?"

"Well, Valerie and Ashley were in that big wreck on the highway. She's in critical condition." I waited. "We need to get to the hospital. Can you and Dad pick up Brian on the way in?"

"Of course." Mom was stunned, then panicked. She called out to Dad, "We need to get to the hospital! Valerie and Ashley were in that bad accident!"

Before running out the door I called Brian. "Valerie and Ashley have been in a bad wreck. Valerie's in critical condition. We don't know about Ashley. Mom and Dad will pick you up on their way." Then I called my husband, Dave, and rushed out the door.

Brian didn't wait for Mom and Dad, but immediately raced to the hospital. Close to 5 p.m., sirens announced Valerie's approaching ambulance. Dr. Mark Donnelly met Brian in the ER. Soon, I and other family members and friends began to gather. We knew nothing until Brian walked into the waiting area, dazed.

"She looks bad." Tears rolled down his cheeks. "Real bad. When I got here, the doctor met me. He said, 'You want to see your wife before we take her back?' Of course, I said yes."

Struggling to compose himself, Brian wiped his nose with his fist. "She was ice cold. Covered in blood. She looked like she was already dead." He looked away for a moment. "Her hand was blue. And…then…I kissed her face. There was blood coming from her nose, all caked up down to her lips." Brian stammered, controlling himself. "They rolled her away, and I came back in here."

The x-rays confirmed it. The extent of Valerie's injuries mocked all hope. Her diaphragm was torn in two, her organs stuffed into her chest cavity. All ribs on her right side were shattered. So was her nose. The impact lacerated her liver, punctured her lung, and dislocated her elbow.

There was more. Valerie had a basilar skull fracture. A small donut-shaped bone called the foramen magnum was cracked. Two interior carotid arteries and part of the brain stem are encased in the bone. Both carotids and the brain stem were damaged, causing Valerie to stroke at least twice after the wreck.

Hours later, Dr. Donnelly came out of surgery to discuss the extent of Valerie's injuries. "She coded twice in the ambulance on the way here," the doctor said. "We have her on life support now."

All the blood seemed to drain from Mom's body. She teetered and fell against a friend. We were all in shock, facing the possibility of life without Valerie.

Valerie was taken to intensive care. Normally, only family members would have been allowed to see her, and only two at a time. But because doctors expected Valerie to die, they gave everyone a turn to visit. The door to her room was practically a revolving door.

When my turn came, the nurse directed me to my sister's room. I entered and wondered. *The nurse must be wrong. That's not Valerie.*

"What room did you say?" I asked the duty nurse.

"That room, where you just were. That's Valerie Paters."

I returned and looked more closely. *How could this be Valerie?* Her head was twice its normal size. A breathing tube jutted from her mouth. A machine beeped as her chest moved up and down. Her eyes were closed. Her body was connected to drains, monitors, and a catheter. My sister's face was contorted by the impossible events of the day.

I was horrified.

In the opinion of the duty nurse, Valerie was already gone. She wasn't there. The life supports were all that stood between her and death. I didn't know any of this at the time. I only knew what God told me—to pray my sister would live, here on planet Earth. Only later would I understand what my prayers meant where Valerie was.

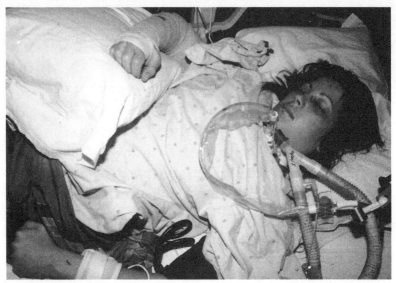

Valerie on life support in ICU

From Earth to Heaven (Valerie)

I stood up. After hours trapped in the Jeep, I was free and feeling no pain. I took deep breaths and looked around. Except for its brightness, the place seemed familiar. I should have been confused but I wasn't. It was like walking through my front door after a long, hard day.

The atmosphere buzzed. Joy filled my body. My feet wanted to dance. I felt connected to the current of life itself, and thought I might burst from it. My thoughts and hopes shot forth. They could not be expressible in words, and didn't need to be. Language was too small, too inadequate for the glory of the place.

Someone was behind me, coming toward me. Or was I being carried to Him? Blinding light swept around my feet and moved upward, warm and washing away my weariness. It seemed as though the sun was rising quickly behind me. As I turned to see it, I was overtaken in its penetrating rays. The glow seemed ready to consume me and make me one with itself.

The luminous rays formed someone who deliberately approached and beckoned to me. I knew that if I got closer, I could unwrap the light and find who I was looking for. Then I collided with Him. His eyes were ocean blue. His hair seemed golden brown but with iridescent wisps. His face was so radiant, I could not look straight into it.

How can I describe what I saw? Only in terms of how His countenance made me feel. It was as though the most exquisite moments of my lifetime were immersed in His expression. Every former joy I felt but could not express showed in His face.

In an instant, my whole life was both fulfilled and of no consequence. There were no loose ends. They would not have mattered anyway. My earthly experiences had resolved in perfect, satisfying sense.

"It's You!" I exclaimed as I put my hands to His face.

The shimmering air moved as I reached toward Him. The atmosphere was phosphorescent. Then I noticed the hum of His body, as though He generated the energy of paradise. It was intense and seemed to hold Him in a comprehensible form. Made of light, He could dissolve into it or expand to the outer reaches of space in an explosion of shooting stars.

Suddenly I was pulled irresistibly into Him, freefalling into His love. My heart knew His. His heart caressed mine. Emotion to emotion. Joy to joy. No words needed. Colors beyond fathoming. Tumbling euphorically, laughing and liberated. Completed! Ravished by my Lord.

Once we were set right again, He looked at me and fell into my being—I in Him, and He in me. I was immersed in happiness. Peals of laughter must have rung through heaven as Jesus, without speaking, showed me the wonders of His love.

5

TWO DIFFERENT WORLDS

Hope from the Unseen (Cheryl)

On that Monday night, Sandi Harris had the three-to-eleven shift at Flagstaff Medical Center. Soon after coming on duty, nurses were notified of the pileup and told to prepare for multiple admissions. Sandi and the others got their existing patients settled so they could focus on the onslaught.

But nothing happened. There were no admissions.

On Tuesday evening, Sandi saw my mom in a hospital corridor. They knew each other from church. "What are you doing in the hospital, Frances?"

"My daughter and granddaughter were in that accident yesterday," she offered.

"Oh, no!" Sandi was shocked. After the announcement during her Monday shift, she'd heard little more about the wreck. "How are they?"

"Ashley's injuries aren't as severe as her mom's," said Mom. "She got knocked about real good, but she's going to be okay."

"And your daughter?"

"Valerie's in intensive care with massive injuries," said my mother. "We're still waiting to hear more."

Sandi had worked in ICU for years. Seeing so many deaths was depressing. It burned her out. But she decided to spend her break with us in the ICU waiting area anyway. When she arrived, we were laughing and talking loudly. She admitted wanting to shush us.

When Mom saw Sandi, she hurried over to her. "Did you hear? Valerie's going to make it! She's going to be all right!" She was gushing. "Do you want to see her?"

"No, that's okay." Sandi had no desire to step through the ICU doors.

"No!" insisted Mom. "Go!" She gave Sandi a little push forward.

Not wanting to seem uncaring, Sandi looked for Valerie's nurse, Sally, with whom she'd worked for several years.

"Hi, Sally. I'm with the family of Valerie Paters. Her mother told me Valerie is going to be okay."

Sally was stunned. "No, she's not."

"Oh?" Sandi was confused.

"The woman has sheared carotids, a severely lacerated liver, multiple broken ribs, and damage to her diaphragm. She's in danger of further strokes and we can't even administer anticoagulants."

Sandi knew what that meant. The carotids are the brain's main source of oxygen. The shearing led to clotting. That's how the body counteracts blood loss. But the clots were also dangerous. Heparin therapy would alleviate the problem but, with so many other injuries, it would also exacerbate internal bleeding. It was a no-win situation.

"Then you're saying—"

"That the patient is being kept alive for donor material." Those were the cold, hard facts. It was part of what Sandi hated about ICU. "Do you want to see her?"

"No," was all Sandi could say.

Nauseated, Sandi walked back to the waiting area where everyone was still celebrating. *Where did Frances get the idea that her daughter was going to be okay?* Valerie is essentially dead. Her chart said it: *ventilator dependent.* In other words, Valerie was not there.

Mom rushed toward Sandi, who stopped her and asked, "What did the doctors tell you?"

Sandi was surprised when Mom recited the litany of Valerie's injuries. Mom knew nothing of the donor protocols, but she was perfectly aware of her daughter's condition. "But Jesus told us He has healed her!" Mom said.

What? Sandi was a Christian, but she thought this was too much. In Valerie's case, He'd have to revive her from the dead.

"Well, I hope He has." Sandi hadn't seen God do much. Nor had she asked much of Him.

Meanwhile, Valerie lay quiet. Doctors checked her glassy eyes for signs of life. Nurses moved her lifeless limbs. Paperwork was prepared so Brian could authorize organ donations before life supports were removed. And we sat vigil beside her bed.

All the while Valerie could not have been more alive.

In the River with Jesus (Valerie)

Standing before Jesus, I was in ecstasy. Energy shook the foundations of eternity and charged my being. It was hard to stand still.

"Valerie." My name rumbled through His lips as if He called to me from within a waterfall. It echoed through heaven, going on and on. "Don't you know how much I love you?"

Jesus lifted His arms to emphasize His love. Their brilliance was incomprehensible. Like cosmic sparklers, they shot fiery light each time He moved.

Jesus loved me and knew my name! There was a Valerie only He had reached. I brought none of Earth's residue to heaven. There was no flesh to hide my shame or my imperfect heart. I was clean, innocent, virginal, perfect. Jesus thought me beautiful. His love perfected me.

Like a bridegroom with his bride, Jesus moved closer and put His hands on my head. From His palms came oil thick and sparkling like warm honey. It flowed down onto my face, neck, and shoulders, and continued till it spilled on my feet. The liquid gold turned my skin iridescent. I thought it took years, but maybe it was moments. Time didn't matter. If I stayed forever, I would only want more.

And, oh—the river! Crystal blue waters cascaded from a light brighter than the sun. Lush green plants and big leafy trees stood on its banks. Butterflies landed on gigantic fruit hanging from branches that arched the river. Melodies from harps, pianos, horns, and drums hung in the atmosphere like symphonies applauding the King of heaven. The songs were more felt than heard, but somehow I knew them.

The river seemed alive. Its emerald banks brushed my ankles. My new form had sharpened senses. Flowers spewed the scent of orange blossoms. Colors burst along the riverbanks. Shrubs rose up as if to greet me.

The river drew me in like a magnet. One moment I was on its banks; the next, I was midstream with Jesus splashing me. I didn't know what to think. He splashed me again, and it was on. We played like children. Without a word, I understood that Jesus didn't want me on the sidelines watching other people having fun. Physical age was meaningless in heaven, but He remembered the heartbroken kid who couldn't walk. He knew she still needed to play.

Breathing and moving like a mermaid, I went under, over, and through the water chasing Jesus. He chased me, too. It was cleansing, purifying. Former hurts were washed away. New, holy memories took their place.

Joy! Joy! Joy! The river sang it, and I thought I heard the trees clap their hands.[1]

Left Behind (Cheryl)

Strapped on a conveyor belt, Ashley awoke to a knocking sound and bright lights.

"Lie still, honey," a nurse was saying. "You've been in an accident. This is a CAT scan."

Too sleepy to stay awake for more, Ashley closed her eyes until Wednesday. Then, as I stroked her hair and bent down close to her face, my niece heard my voice.

"Hi, honey,"

Ashley answered with a moan, prying open one eye, and then another. I watched her sort through the memories. *There was a black truck. I remember a black truck.* She mumbled, and became startled, pulling tubes from her hands and arms. She wanted out of wherever she was.

"You can't do that, Ashley." I patted her hands. "You've been in an accident. You're in intensive care."

Her tongue was swollen and unruly. "What's wrong with my tongue? It feels weird."

She turned toward me, but pain caught her. Her hip hurt, her arm was in a sling, and there was something wrong with her stomach. That much she knew.

"Your teeth are a little chipped, but they can be fixed." I smiled, maybe too kindly.

Ashley looked at her wrist.

"It's fractured." I blinked back tears. "Your bladder ruptured and the left side of your pelvis is fractured."

Trying to understand, Ashley touched the gash on her cheek.

"You had a concussion, too, Ashley. You've been pretty much out of it since they brought you to the hospital."

"What day is it?" Ashley asked with difficulty.

"Wednesday."

She was fourteen now, and had slept through her birthday. Staying awake was hard. So she didn't.

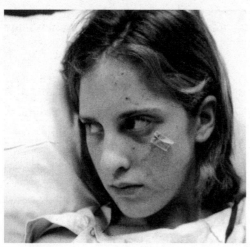

Ashley in ICU

By Thursday morning Ashley was well enough to be in a regular room. It was filled with flowers, and a woman in another bed. Being left alone with a stranger was tough in Ashley's current condition. Her world had turned surreal. She kept seeing the black rig coming at her. Flashbacks catapulted her into a loneliness she couldn't shake.

When I came in, Ashley asked for a mirror to see her face, not just feel it. What she saw was hard to take. She fought the tears and put the mirror down.

"What about Mom? Where's Mom? Nobody's said anything about her." Ashley's face turned red as she awaited my answer.

∽

By Tuesday night I was completely exhausted. Everyone was; yet no one wanted to leave. It seemed like everyone Valerie had ever known visited her, as if to see her alive one last time. Ashley's friends came, too. That day, her condition was upgraded from critical to stable. She had no life-threatening injuries. She was going to pull through.

A local congregation had decided to pray for Valerie's recovery. She had become a kind of celebrity in town. All the local papers, even outside of Flagstaff, treated the wreck as front-page news.

"How should we pray for your sister?" the pastor of the praying congregation asked.

"Valerie will live and not die and proclaim the works of the Lord."[2] I more decreed it than answered the man's question.

"Then she'll live," he said. And that was that.

Yet nothing changed to speak of. Valerie's prognosis was horrific. To believe she would live was to defy reality. Death hung over her as she lay intubated…her eyes fixed and glassy.

Early Wednesday, I left the waiting area and walked to the hospital chapel down the hall. It was hard to imagine Valerie getting up and walking out of the hospital. I fell into a pew and closed my eyes. *I need to focus on something besides the hopelessness of all this.*

I grasped for perspective—God's, not mine. Clearly, I needed to get still and listen to His thoughts instead of the negative predictions being presented to me.

"Oh, Lord Jesus…" I breathed out His name and felt drawn into His presence.

I waited.

"You need to pray her back. She's with Me, and doesn't want to leave." I knew that inner voice.

Pray for my sister to leave His presence, and return to the broken, swollen body lying in the hospital bed? I couldn't imagine Valerie opening her eyes to this life after seeing Jesus' face. Why would she want to see what her body had become, and how dependent it was on machines?

That seems unfair, Jesus.

Little did I know how hard Valerie would fight to stay with Him.

Witnessing the River, in Prayer (Cheryl)

Late that day as I sat in Valerie's room, a friend from our prayer group dropped in. I was emotionally exhausted but unwilling to leave my sister's side. "You and your sister are so close in spirit," remarked the friend. "You'll have to be the one who fights to get her back."

When the friend left I rested my head on the edge of Valerie's bed. Weary, I said, "Lord, please give me strength for this battle."

As I headed out to the waiting room, I hoped there were people there who knew how to pray. I looked back at Valerie, and shut the door.

Six people followed me into the chapel. "We've got to pray her back," I said.

They understood. Except for us, the chapel was empty, so the women spread out across pews and on the floor. Face down on the carpet, I pleaded with God. In what felt like a war zone, I forgot about those praying beside me. Praying Valerie back was my assignment.

In the distance I heard the sound of rushing water. My bare feet touched warm round stones that formed a path through ferns and daffodils. Everything growing there seemed illumined from within. The sky was exquisitely aqua and met the horizon in a brilliant blaze of color.

Light made rainbows as I moved my hands. The sound of the river grew louder and drew me forward in a holy dance. I heard voices, like children frolicking. I ran, or more like floated, toward the sounds of playful splashing.

The rush of the river was deafening, yet the water was iridescent and clear as glass. There in midstream was Valerie, dressed in a translucent gown of royal purple. She was unaware of me at first. She was busy scooping up huge handfuls of water and throwing them at one who could only be Jesus.

Laughter chimed through heaven. Like someone peeping through a keyhole, I watched Jesus and Valerie play. It was a marvel—who could believe it? Then Valerie turned and looked at me. There was recognition, yet she was unready for me to join her. Valerie was complete now. Whether she still related to me as sister, I don't know. I was more of a fleeting interruption to her play with Jesus.

"Taste!" Valerie laughed, splashing water onto my face. "Taste and see that the Lord is good!"[3]

Sweet nectar flowed down my cheeks and into my mouth. It made me hungry for heaven and for Jesus. From here I must pray her back? How will she ever bear it?

Then the scene vanished and I was aware of being back in the chapel. Anguished, I stood up and prayed for my sister's return, knowing it meant her departure from paradise and her return to a broken body. All I could see was Valerie's face.

Then I realized I was lying on a precipice. My hands grasped Valerie's as she dangled from the edge. If I let go, she would be gone from us forever.

My sister's eyes were desperate as she screamed, "Let me go!"

The cruelty was clear. I ignored my sister's plea. I held even more tightly to her hands because God told me to pray her back.

"Valerie, it's going to be better when you get back. He's promised it." I would not release my grip, despite her fierce struggle.

"Let me go! Let me go!"

She strained against my hold for what seemed like hours. When a flicker of resignation showed in her eyes, I held tighter. I was calling Valerie back from His presence.

Complete in Him (Valerie)

Enormous, ornate gates stood before me, light spiking from their bronzy finish. They were opened wide, as though we were expected. A walkway wound through myriad landscapes and elevations. The beauty took me in and joy surged inside me. It was beyond anything imaginable on Earth.

Dazzling hues stretched as far as the eye could see. There was a forested area through which a mighty river flowed. Trees on either side of it were bent heavily with fruit. Orange blossoms and sap scented the air.

Then I saw a blanket stretched across a broad expanse. A patchwork of colors moved with the wind. Like an impressionist painting, each color merged into part of the larger landscape. Soon, I understood that it was a field of flowers. Roses, asters, jasmine, daffodils, irises, petunias, pansies, and birds of paradise were perfectly arranged. Huge petals of flowers I couldn't name played in the breeze and made me want to laugh and spin in delight.

When I turned to look again, Jesus was beside me. Beneath our feet was the warm, sandy oasis. The air was humid. The water was a mirror in which I saw my reflection, but also my thoughts and memories. We seemed to relax there for a long while. Images of past hurts and memories were drawn from my mind. Events and my perceptions of them were revealed. Jesus reached for them as scenes He could hold in His hands. Then He rearranged them and changed my thinking so that I saw as He saw. The past events and perceptions were then burned away in a quick burst of light.

Thoughts were transferred from my mind to His, without using language. Words were unnecessary in heaven. He revealed my religious spirit without having to show me the details. I can't say how, but He turned my thoughts around as though solving a math problem I'd answered incorrectly. He showed me how to think perfectly, and easily.

Jesus reached for me. I leaned in toward Him as He touched my heart. Until I felt the gentle pressure of His palm, I did not realize the pain I had inside me. My heart had many fractures, and Jesus wanted to heal them. The process was not grueling—no having to recite every injustice I'd experienced and then process it. As each memory was covered with oil from His hand, it simply vanished. Nothing mattered but His touch.

Jesus did not cleanse my memories or chastise my heart. The oasis was for restoration, refreshing, and replenishing. I was still myself, but renewed.

Notes

1. See Isaiah 55:12.
2. See Psalms 118:17.
3. See Psalms 34:8.

6

THE BROKEN BODY AND THE BLESSINGS

Sharing the Cup (Cheryl)

For months the Thursday group prayed for the Church. We knew what the Bible says: After Jesus returns to Earth, heaven will host the great Marriage Supper of the Lamb. His Bride must be made ready, dressing in white linen and perfecting her heart.

Aware of great divisions within the Church, we prayed for two things: a vision of how to prepare the Bride for her royal wedding and a revelation of Jesus' passion. We wanted to understand what He experienced on the cross for us. Little did I know on the fourth night of Valerie's hospitalization, that she would become, for me, a picture of both.

The ICU waiting area was full of people. I noted (angrily, I admit) that many of them had not been there when Valerie needed them in the past. Now, on Thursday night, they wanted to see her one last time.

Did it take this for all of you to realize how precious she is to you? My patience was thin. I hated that my little sister was a spectacle to them. Besides, I was called to pray the night through at her bedside. *How can I do that, Father? There are too many people around her!*

The family was exhausted. Mom, Dad, and Brian had been there every minute just like I had. We needed rest but felt guilty about leaving while Valerie's life hung in the balance. Yet rest was necessary. We would have to sleep eventually.

"I'll stay the night," I said. It was time for us to take shifts, and it was my opportunity to be alone with my sister.

Valerie's room was quiet. No sound except the machines. I dropped heavily into a rocking chair, wondering how many tired souls had collapsed there before me.

Jesus, I will pray all night for her. For the first two hours, there was much to pray. As though purging, I emptied out my concerns for Valerie's battered body. But as the hours dragged on, my eyes drooped.

"Can you not pray with Me one hour?"[1] Jesus asked His disciples this question in the garden of Gethsemane on the night He was arrested. I understood the question more than I ever had. *Don't fall asleep, Cheryl. Pray!*

I shook myself awake and walked over to Valerie, knowing she was somewhere else. I remembered the desperation in her eyes as she dangled from the precipice. Conflicted again by the cruelty of not letting her go, yet sure that God wanted her to live and not die, I paced the room and prayed for her return.

Early Friday morning, a nurse came to feed Valerie through the tube inserted into her side. The food was a slimy, pungent liquid.

"May I taste it?" I asked. "I want to experience everything she is experiencing."

"Really?" The nurse was incredulous.

"Yes."

"It tastes really horrible. I tried it once myself." He grimaced as he poured me a tiny portion. It smelled rancid. Determined to share my sister's cross, I tasted it.

"Yuck!" I could not swallow it. I spat it into the sink.

The nurse was right. Yet I felt guilty, like I should drink of Valerie's cup the way Jesus asked His disciples to drink of His.

The hours began to drag on. As my body gave way to fatigue, I shook myself back into prayer. I moved, paced, and did anything necessary to stay in the battle and fight.

At dawn the nurse returned with towels and fresh sheets. "It's time for her bath," he said. Then he paused to look at me. "You want to bathe her?"

"Yes, but how?"

"Gently remove her clothes. Here is some soapy water and a sponge. Ring the service bell if you need help. I'll leave you with her." He tiptoed out.

Valerie's body would have been familiar to me when it was whole. In its new form, it was foreign. Carefully, I lifted the blankets and sheets. *Oh, God.* My sister was crushed and lacerated. Blood pumped into and out of her tiny frame. I wiped her face, mindful of her blackened eyes and broken nose. I avoided touching the horribly swollen lips now coated in salve to keep them from bursting open.

It's still hard to believe this is Valerie.

Removing the hospital gown, I surveyed my sister's body. A tube exited from her side. My breath became a sob. "Jesus, this is like Your body when it was taken from the cross."

Tears of grief stung my eyes. In touching Valerie, I seemed to be touching Christ. As I sponged her, her fingers and palms became His. I felt like I was at the tomb, preparing His broken body for burial. Just like Jesus, my sister was bloodied and bruised. The tube in her side reminded me of the spear thrust into His abdomen. I burst into tears knowing Jesus had been pierced for me.

With my arms arched over Valerie and my hands resting on the opposite side of the bed, I sobbed over her body and the body of my Lord. My long hair wiped up my tears as I moved to wash her abdomen. The similarity between Valerie and Jesus was clear to me. Tending her was tending Him. She was almost unrecognizable. He was beaten and stripped of His flesh. No longer did I need a picture of Him hanging naked on the cross. I'd touched His suffering anew.

I washed Valerie's feet last. The scars from her childhood surgeries made me conscious of Christ's pierced hands and feet. Somehow, I was at the foot of His cross. Rubbing her legs and arms with lotion was like anointing Jesus for burial. The very thing the intercessors prayed for, I was beginning to understand and experience. While Jesus was revealing Himself to Valerie in heaven, He was revealing Himself to me on Earth.

I cried uncontrollably as I reached for a fresh gown in which to wrap my sister. I folded her arms into the sleeves and laid it over her, untied. Pulling up the covers around her shoulders, I wept for her woundedness.

As I put the soiled towels in a corner by the door, I whispered, "Thank You, Jesus, for the price You paid so Valerie could be there with You, and I could be here, and both of us could be Yours."

Every few hours the nurse checked Valerie's vital signs. He parted her eyelids and searched inside with a penlight, looking for any signs of cognition. Her unresponsiveness had become routine.

But when he checked again near the end of his shift, he was shocked. "I'm going to get the duty nurse," he said, and hurried out of the room.

Almost before I could wonder what happened, he came back with the registered nurse rushing in behind him. She shined the light into Valerie's eyes and said, "Go get the doctor. I see something going on in there now."

"What's happening?" I asked, my heart pounding. *Valerie must be coming back.*

"There is finally a little brain response," the nurse answered. "We want the doctor to see this, too."

The excited doctor arrived quickly and looked into Valerie's eyes. "Oh, my God! She's in there!" To the nurse he said, "Start decreasing her medication. Let's see if we can wake her up."

Smiling and patting Valerie's shoulder, the doctor said, "Looks like your sister just might come back to us."

Valerie and I were alone again. But everything had changed, in a moment. *What will she be like? What did she see?*

Valerie thanking Dr. Donnelly.

The Mountaintop and the Throne (Valerie)

We were moving fast, or flying, toward a high peak. We approached it with such speed I thought we would crash. But so close to Jesus, so protected by His arm around me, I was safe.

Without effort, we reached the mountain and peered across heaven. I saw spring here and snowy peaks there, the richness of autumn and the shimmering summer, too—all the seasons at their peak.

Jesus and I stood in an atmosphere that glowed like dawn, moist and with thick clouds to cushion me. Under my feet rocks shifted. A voice thundered throughout the realm. Though I could not see Him, I heard God calling out blessings over the heavens and the earth. The sound was loud and penetrating, reverberating into eternity. My cloud of safety lit up with almost blinding light. I knew that, without its covering, I would have been consumed.

"Blessing!" His word resounded. "Blessing here and on the earth!"

Then a thick, palpable goodness permeated the place. I can't tell you how, but it was a sensory fact—a taste, a smell, a touch as real as a strawberry bursting with flavor in my mouth. The reality of God's goodness and love was evident.

As the hurricane of blessing eased, Jesus presented me to the Father. It was unmistakable: God saw me. He looked at me. Here was Valerie, standing beside Christ in a luminous cloud on a mountaintop in eternity. I belonged to my Father. The quiet of the moment told me this. I felt as though I was holding my breath.

Jesus took my hand and led me out from the cloud toward a symphony of indescribable harmonies. The sounds saturated all of paradise. I realized they had been in the background all along. But as we approached from above, the music flowed through me the way blood once flowed through my earthly body. It energized and called me into the heavenly score.

Thousands and hundreds of thousands of angels sang with the saints: "Holy, holy, holy is our God."[2] Exultation overflowed in the purity of the song. Undefiled souls, forgiven, reborn, restored, and perfect uttered their raw devotion. Angels that harmonized with the saints had been created for this unending act of worship.

Rainbow rays shot from the gates surrounding the city of God. They bounced off marble structures like lasers in a light show. Emerald arcs swirled around the throne. Angels sounding shofars and saints with trumpets and other instruments worshiped in perfect unity. They shook the throne room.

Yet I stood apart from it all. No one seemed to see or notice me. I wondered why I did not fully enter in with Jesus. Later, I would learn why. For the moment it was enough to be with Him.

Very close to me, prostrate on heaven's floor was an angel without wings. I knew he had been created for worship because an endless flow of adoration issued from his mouth and wracked his being. The desire to join him made me tremble. God's loving-kindness was thick and transcendent. The sweetness of the moment filled me with love and thankfulness.

The music's volume rose and fell causing the hum from the throne to feed back, yet without sounding painful or out of place. Before me was the power source for the whole universe! It surged with the creative omnipotence that sustains everything.

Heaven is reality! God is enthroned there, surrounded by angelic beings and humans who died knowing Him. My earthly experiences seemed like shadows of what I now saw. I understood what Jesus meant when He said to pray: "Thy kingdom come. Thy will be done, on earth as it is in heaven."[3]

The Hardest Questions of All (Valerie)

I noticed that other guests were dressed in white linen aglow with heaven's light. They sat at a table set for a gigantic feast. Pineapples, apples, melons, strawberries, figs, pomegranates, and fruits I had never seen before were arranged in golden bowls. The food released its fragrance and made me hungry. A rich red liquid flowed from beautiful fountains, into waiting goblets. The guests were chatting, almost noisy in their revelry. It seemed I was an onlooker to a party—a wedding.

Anticipation energized the multiplied thousands at the feast. Guests continued arriving and were greeted warmly as though everyone knew each other and had expected to meet together. For the first time I understood that I was an observer not yet ready to partake with them.

My purple gown shimmered to a bright blue as I moved along the crowd's perimeter. I looked at Jesus and knew—I was going back. He didn't say it then. But the dread of parting told me I was inching closer to the moment I would return to Earth. I danced and twirled in front of Jesus, stalling like a child at bedtime who distracts her father from putting her to sleep.

Jesus watched my gown swirl as I pirouetted for Him. My heart said, "Please don't send me back! Please, let's not think about that!"

I smiled at Him, hoping He would never say what I knew He would. Long ago, He had asked me whether I would die for Him. The thought had been overwhelming. Much more unbearable was the thought of leaving Him. I simply couldn't do it!

As the merriment continued and strains of worship filled my heart, Jesus took my hands and spoke to me. "You can stay if you want to, but you haven't yet finished My purposes for you. I would rather you go back."

As Jesus said those words, I shook my head. "No. I want to stay here with You!" How could I leave?

The longer I was there, the more distressed I became about leaving. Earth was a distant memory. What could be so important there that I must leave Christ to accomplish it? I did not yet know that my body was broken or that I would exchange my present joy for excruciating pain. Even that might be bearable, but parting with Jesus? How could I?

The redeemed in heaven know no tears, but I was a sojourner there. I guess I was allowed to cry. "I will do whatever You ask of me," I said, "but please let me stay with You!"

Jesus spoke gently. He understood what it meant to leave heaven and go down to Earth. He knew separation from His home and from His Father. My tears fell on His fingers as He wiped my face. He did not say, "Not My will but Thine be done,"[4] yet the words sounded in my soul. With my heart devastated, I acquiesced.

As I lay on a double bed in a sparsely furnished room, the brightness of Jesus was dimmed as though to ease me into transition. Melodies flowed from the cool marble walls. The room was serene, like a birthing room. A table and lamp beside the bed came into focus. I knew I had begun my journey back.

With the tender care of a father tucking in his beloved daughter, Jesus spread a light cover over me and stroked my forehead. When He sat down on the bed and held my hand, I fell into a deep sleep. It was interrupted when He got up and paced the room. He then returned to my side and I slept. Again, He paced, as if waiting for a precise moment—not of my death, but of my return to life on Earth.

With my eyes slightly opened, I watched Jesus memorize my face the way a mother studies the face of her newborn child. He took in every detail. I realized that He would miss me, and that I was precious to Him, as I am even now. His eyes narrowed on mine. His love was tinged with the sadness of our temporary parting.

Then I began falling, spiraling fast through time and space. With a groan I was forced through what felt like a sieve. Thoughts rushed toward me. Once again, I began dropping fast. Confusion swirled back into my body.

Thud!

I felt unspeakable pain and heard machines beeping and moaning. One fed me. One pushed my battered lungs up and down against broken ribs. My eyes were swollen nearly shut. My body was made immovable by slings and bandages.

Still suspended between there and here, I heard Jesus' now familiar voice say, "This is My beloved Bride."

I was returned to my role in a cosmic drama. The Bride of Christ, His Church, must not have been ready for her wedding day, because, surely, I should never have risen from my bed in ICU. But I did. And soon, He would call me to pray for His Bride to be made ready.

Notes

1. See Matthew 26:40.
2. See Revelation 4:8.
3. See Matthew 6:10.
4. See Luke 22:42.

7

LIGHT OVERCOMING DARKNESS

My Sister's Road Back (Cheryl)

"You need to leave now," the new nurse told me on Friday morning. "It's time for our shift change."

The long night was over. A glimmer of hope strengthened my walk to the waiting room. Pastor John and two women from the Thursday group were there. Something in me broke when I saw them, and I fell at their feet, sobbing.

Are you going to take her after all, Lord? This seemed to be the root of my desperation. But I also mourned the death of Jesus and His separation from the Father. And I ached over the previous night's revelation of His suffering.

Suddenly, I saw Jesus' face as He stood with outstretched arms. "This is the day I've longed for," He said. "I long to see My Bride made whole."

My grief turned into joy, and I lifted my hands in praise.

My pastor knew nothing about my night of prayer, so my behavior was perplexing, and maybe a little embarrassing to him. He bowed his head and prayed until my emotions subsided. Eventually, I wiped my tears and sat beside him.

I was beyond exhaustion. Praying my sister back from death was daunting. But my behavior involved more than that. We intercessors had unusual ways of expressing what God revealed. John knew that from experience. Yet, it probably looked kooky at times.

The prophets of old could have explained it. God told them to do some *very* weird things. Ezekiel had to lie on his side for months on end. Hosea was instructed to marry a prostitute. Jeremiah was called to weep.

Now John understood, too. He said, "Cheryl, I've learned a lot about intercession from you during this time." Then he patted my hand and cleared his throat. "Do you remember last Sunday when the group was praying in the classroom?"

"Yes."

"Remember how I asked you to leave before you were done praying?" John squirmed a little. "I've wondered this week…if I hadn't been in such a hurry…if you had finished praying, maybe this wreck wouldn't have happened."

"Don't even go there, John. The accident was not your fault."

Then I told him about my vigil. He put his arm around my shoulder and tried to take in my experience with Christ's broken body. "Cheryl, you need to ponder these things in your heart before you share them with others."

"I know," I whispered. "I know." There were so many missing puzzle pieces. It would take time to really grasp what had been revealed.

Just then Brian, Mom, and Dad returned.

"How is she this morning?" asked Mom.

"The doctor thinks he saw some brain activity," I said. "He's hopeful that Valerie's coming back."

"Really?" Brian could not control the tears.

"You look exhausted, Cheryl," said Mom. "Go home and get some rest."

"I think I will," I said, digging for my car keys.

On the way home, I remembered something God had shown me earlier that week. I was praying alone in the chapel when I felt myself taken up into a sphere above the Earth. There I floated free and watched the movements of our neighboring planets. As I focused on Earth, I saw a dot coming from the east. It grew brighter and larger as it neared Earth.

The dot consisted of golden bands of light. They were hundreds of miles wide and illuminated all of space as they wrapped themselves around our sphere. The bright bands swirled noisily, faster and faster. A kind of music emanated from them—not like the whirring sound of galaxies, but more harmonic and glorious than a symphony.

Deeper, richer sounds issued from inside the light mass. It was God's glory embracing His creation as He promised the restoration of all things. I didn't know that by week's end He would guide Valerie back to her broken earthly body. But now that signs of life had reappeared in her eyes, the vision made sense.

When I turned down my street, my house welcomed me like an old friend would. All tension vaporized, and total exhaustion took over. I took a hot bath and fell asleep.

Becoming a Metaphor

In mid-afternoon I woke up abruptly, eager to return to the hospital. I rifled through my closet, certain that I was hearing the Lord's instructions. I was to wear black pants, a white shirt, and my pearl necklace.

Light has overcome the darkness. I was to become a metaphor.

At a florist's shop on the way, I bought lilies and roses and knew I would also find the perfect vase. As though a spotlight were trained on it, I saw a clear glass vase alone on a shelf. Swirled around it were bright, white bands that caught the light and reminded me of the vision of God's glory.

Puzzle pieces were coming together! Several pastors who visited Valerie regularly all believed that God was doing more than just healing her. The vase beautifully confirmed the fact that, although some pieces were still missing, the picture was becoming clearer day by day.

After the florist, I picked up Anne, a prayer team member. When she came to the door, she smiled and shook her head. "God told you what to wear, didn't He?"

"Yes," I replied.

"He told me the same thing, but I didn't do it."

That night, I left the flowers close to Valerie. She was still in a distant place, but I was confident she would return. The vase was a reminder that the same God who was restoring her to life would one day restore all things.

Mom's Life in the Balance (Ashley)

On Thursday morning I was alone in my hospital room. Aunt Cheryl had told me the day before that my mom was severely injured and in ICU. She didn't mention life support or Mom's eyes being fixed like a dead person's.

"Would you like to visit your mother today?" asked my nurse.

"Okay," I said, having no clue what to expect.

The nurse helped me get into a wheelchair, and made small talk. "I'm sure your mom will be glad to see you."

The doors to ICU closed behind us. I remember thinking that I might get to talk to Mom, and even hold her hand. Then we entered her room. Everything I thought was wrong. Two nurses held my mom's stiff, bluish legs up in the air while massaging them. A hose was attached to Mom's throat. Wires and tubes came out of her body. Machines cranked to keep her alive. Christian music played quietly.

Then I saw Mom's eyes. My breath shortened. My heart raced. *She's not in there. Mom's not in there. She's dead. They brought me here to see her one last time.* Her empty stare told me more than I wanted to know. The nurses were massaging a dead woman who used to be my mother.

A wail shot out from within me, as I exploded in pain. The nurses suddenly realized the visit was a bad idea. They rushed me back to my room, but it was too late. I could not erase the images from my mind.

I don't know how I'm going to live. Mom isn't there. She's gone. I don't know what to do.

So much had happened since seeing the black truck coming at us. The movie played over and over in my mind, even as my future was coming apart. *I can't live alone with Dad. Maybe with Aunt Cheryl and Uncle Dave, but not alone with Dad. I have to figure this out. I have to figure out my whole life.*

I was now a girl without her mom. *I'd better get used to it—feel it now so I'll never have to feel it again.*

Like my mother before me, I pushed down the pain and separated from it. I didn't visit my mother again during the five days before I was discharged into Aunt Cheryl's care.

Pain and the Scent of Heaven (Valerie)

I was vaguely aware of music playing. The comforting worship touched me deeply. It was the last thing I heard before sedation carried me off, and the first thing I heard when I awakened.

I felt nothing but pain. My first movements took my breath away and caused my head to pound. Waves of nausea rolled through me. My right hand would not move. My entire right side ignored my commands. My vision was blurred to near blindness. Blinking did not help.

There was no doubt: I was alive. But I was disoriented. Questions scrolled through my mind: *Where am I? How did I get here?* I shut my eyes and saw a mighty stream with tall trees on either bank. Water was rushing and splashing. Then I recalled His radiant face. "Valerie, don't you know how much I love you?"

The question gave purpose to my pain. *He sent me back, but only after I was sure that He loved me!*

"He loves me." My heart decreed it with each reentry to consciousness. "Jesus really loves me." Elation from that thought brought me peace. I was fresh from Jesus' presence, and He was all that mattered. My circumstances were real and terrible, yet I basked in Jesus' love.

As the days passed, I became more aware of faces looking into mine. During brief periods of consciousness, I heard familiar voices in my ear. I felt Cheryl's hand in mine, Mom stroking my hair back, Dad kissing me on the cheek. Vague questions came to mind. *What happened to me? Why am I here?*

"Welcome back, Valerie."

It was Cheryl. I recognized her through the haze. *Where have I been?* I wanted to ask, but could not.

Instead, I went back to sleep and searched my subconscious for His hand holding mine. The first thing I remembered from heaven was the bed I slept on before Jesus sent me back. I felt the gentle pressure of Him sitting beside me. His presence was abiding, even in ICU.

"Nothing is impossible when we put our trust in God." As I drifted in and out of consciousness, those words played on Cheryl's CD player. Nurses gathered at my door to listen. One asked Cheryl, "Have you noticed the scent in the room?"

"Not really," said Cheryl, although the question did not surprise her.

"We've talked about it," the nurse continued. "It's fragrant. Like perfume."

Cheryl thought Christ left His scent on me, the way a woman leaves hints of perfume on the people she hugs.

Sandi Harris heard the good news about my progress and was awed by it. As a nurse, she understood my condition. She knew how far gone I was and how the odds were stacked against me. Yet I was alive and recovering! *Only God could've done this. He has the final say.*

Months later Sandi told Mom how she'd seen God do things she had never seen Him do before. She felt her heart soften as my physical condition improved.

∾

Communication came gradually. Tubes still connected my body to machines. Each day, intravenous medications were cut back, and the pain grew more intense. At that point, I still had no memory of the collision and little understanding of how I landed in the hospital.

Now, heaven was more real to me than Earth. Whispers from my experience with Christ lingered. Phrases like "He stood between the living and the dead"[1] played in my head all day long. I supposed that it meant Jesus was interceding for me as I lay in bed.

And always I heard, "Valerie, don't you know how much I love you?"

I was as ecstatic as the first time I heard Jesus say it. Physically, I was still a mess. Every square inch of me screamed with pain. But,

Jesus loved me. He *really* loved me. Knowing that overwhelmed all else. When finally I could whisper something, all I wanted to say was "Jesus loves me. He *really* loves me."

Note

1. See Numbers 16:48.

8

One Step at a Time

Welcome to Therapy (Valerie)

Many days passed before I was sufficiently weaned from medication to move around. Every movement was still excruciating. I remained intubated, and a large feeding tube protruded from my abdomen.

I knew *where* I was, but other details were beyond me.

The duty nurse began filling in the blanks. "It's Monday, April 3, 2000. We are going to get your body going today. A physical therapist is coming by. We need to get you up and out of that bed."

Her smile challenged my disbelief. *Out of bed? Really?* I couldn't imagine how that would work. My right side would not move and a sling weighed down my right arm. Even slight movements in bed were unmanageable.

The irony bordered on hilarity. At least once a day I remembered Jesus calling me His Bride. Wasn't she supposed to be without spot or blemish? And wasn't I one bruised and broken being? To top it off, the prayer group was still seeking a revelation of the Bride. They had not yet heard all that God had revealed to Cheryl and me, or how He used our trial to do it.

Nevertheless, it was April 3rd—and the Bride was about to get moving!

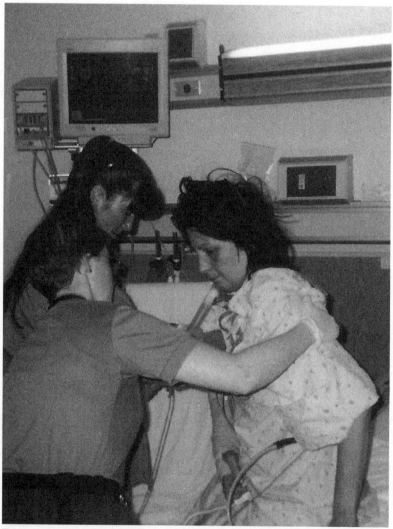

Therapy in ICU: sitting up for 45 minutes

~

Around the end of April, when I was no longer intubated, the speech therapist arrived with a booklet and some medication. Mom and Dad were with me as an old, familiar knot formed in my stomach. Therapy was not new to me. Therapists had manipulated my feet after my childhood surgeries. I'd learned long ago how to swallow the pain in silence.

Yet, today's challenges would exceed my prior experiences.

"I'll bet you would like to eat again, wouldn't you, Valerie?" As she spoke, the therapist removed long swabs from their packaging.

I nodded. *You bet I want to eat again!*

"I'm going to swab the back of your throat. It will stimulate your reflex to swallow. Your throat has gotten kind of lazy, and we don't want anything you drink to slip into your lungs."

The woman looked at Dad and explained, "This needs to be done several times a day. Would you like to learn how to do it?"

"Of course," Dad replied. He watched as the therapist moved the swab from the soft palate down the middle of my tongue.

The swabs tasted like lemon juice, and caused saliva to fill my mouth. My throat responded, weakly at first. It was my first taste of anything since the wreck, and I liked it.

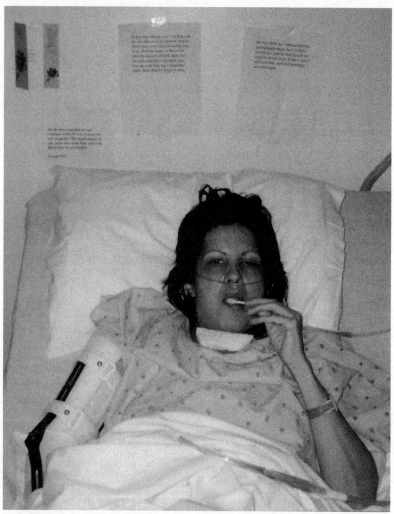

Upgraded, out of ICU, and still on feeding tube—Valerie enjoys a lemon swab.

The speech therapist switched gears. "Now, let's work with some flash cards." She drew a ring of cards from her pocket. "Do you think you could name the items pictured?"

I nodded. *I hope so.*

Holding up a card she said, "What is this, Valerie?"

I couldn't make it out at first. Then I realized that I couldn't see the card well enough to identify it. It was as though a flash bulb had just gone off in my face.

"I still can't see…very well," I whispered.

"Do you usually wear glasses?"

I was unsure how to answer, so Mom rescued me. "She does. They're right over there."

Dad reached for the glasses and set them on my face.

"Okay. Let's try again." The speech therapist flipped to the next card.

"Can you…hold..it…closer?"

I could almost make out the image. "It's a cat."

"Good!" She flipped another card.

I knew it was a bicycle, but I could not get the word to my mouth.

"Do you know what it is, Valerie?"

I nodded.

She prompted me. "It starts with *bi*—"

"Bi-cy-cle." *There it is!*

The cards wore me out till I felt dizzy and sick to my stomach.

"I think that's enough for now," the therapist announced.

Reading her face was difficult, but I tried. Did I pass or fail? Am I too tired to care?

When the therapist left, Mom combed my hair and wiped my face with a cool cloth. The swelling had subsided, but my eyes were still blackened and the bridge of my nose was still tender. The touch of the cloth was painful. Even my ears hurt.

After lunch Judy, the physical therapist, arrived. "This afternoon we are going to sit up. How does that sound?"

I tried to smile.

Two aides assisted, one on either side of the bed. They slowly raised my head and rearranged my pillows. "We are going to help you sit up on the side of the bed, Valerie."

Each aide gently pushed my back away from the pillows. Then one aide supported my back while the other moved my legs toward the edge of the bed. I felt wrenched in two.

"Is this too uncomfortable?" asked Judy.

I managed to bite my upper lip and groan, but not quit.

"We have to get you out of bed if you're going to walk out of here!" urged the nurse. "Now, take your time."

The pain was partly caused by displaced organs that scrambled and bumped into one another. My right side was heavy. The sling on my arm felt like cement. Three people maneuvered me one inch at a time. Finally, I sat on the edge of the bed. My feet dangled for the first time in weeks!

The effort left me woozy. *How could sitting up have been so easy before the accident?*

"Good girl," said Judy. "How does that feel?"

It felt like I might pass out, or even die!

We were not nearly done. Judy bent down in front of me and pulled my left leg straight out from the bed. She then bent and stretched it, and eased it down again. She repeated the exercise with my right leg. The leg movements increased the pressure on my abdomen. The need for deeper breaths caused my lungs to expand against my broken ribs.

"I...need...to...lie...back...down," I whispered.

My ashen face signaled quitting time. "We'll try again tomorrow." Judy patted me reassuringly and rang for the floor nurse.

∼

Later that day, Cheryl dropped by. She looked so pretty and so normal.

"Hi, Valerie!" she said cheerfully. "How was your day?"

"Tough. Looked…at…pictures."

"That sounds fun."

"Tried…to…sit…up."

"Wow! I bet that wasn't easy," Cheryl cringed for me.

"How do I…look?" I asked, unsure I wanted the answer.

"Like a bride!" teased Cheryl.

My heart thumped. "This is My Bride," He said. Wondering what my experience meant and how it all fit, I had not yet shared what He said. "I've…seen…some things," I said.

"I've seen some things, too, Valerie," she whispered. "I know it's hard for you to speak. I can hardly wait for us to share what we've seen!"

I think I smiled with the anticipation of telling my sister about heaven. *I know something you don't know.*

As the days and weeks passed, therapy became more bearable and, always, the Holy Spirit comforted me. Often, I closed my eyes to feel His breath on my face and His arms around my waist. My

Love was there, touching my broken body and whispering His devotion. I was head over heels for Him and homesick for heaven.

In the second week of April, Judy spoke earnestly. "Today, let's stand and bend your left leg upward."

She was asking the impossible.

Nevertheless, aides put a soft orthopedic shoe on my right foot and a white sneaker on my left. Slowly, I strained to stand. Then I teetered and leaned into Judy, who said, "Okay, Valerie, let's lift up that left leg a little."

I tried to move my right leg.

"No." She tapped my left leg. "This one."

Again I looked toward my right leg, and tried to move it.

"The one with the white shoe, Valerie," instructed Judy, while pointing. "Let's try to move that foot up a little." Then she took my calf in her hands, gently bending the knee and lifting my foot slightly.

"Now, you try."

Judy remained bent over, watching as I coaxed my brain to direct my foot. My teeth were clenched, and finally—

There. It moved!

"Once more," said Judy.

I don't know if I can. But I did.

"Good!" Judy exclaimed as my left foot lifted a quarter inch off the floor. "We'll try again tomorrow."

The process took an hour. Cheryl dropped by later, but I was asleep. Weary, she lay down on the cot where Dad usually spent the night, and dozed off.

I awoke startled. "Cheryl!"

"Yes, Valerie?"

"I…saw…Him."

"Him who?" Her look told me she already knew.

"I…saw…Jesus." I remembered falling into Him and feeling warm oil flow down my body.

"I saw Jesus, too, Valerie." There was a knowing in Cheryl's eyes. "It was a fight to get you back. I had to really fight in prayer."

I tried connecting the pieces to understand what my sister meant. *Cheryl was there.* I smiled at the thought of it. *Cheryl saw Jesus, too!*

I was not quite ready to declare the puzzle solved, so I closed my eyes and went back to sleep.

A Long, Long Way from Paradise (Cheryl)

"Am I acting okay?" Valerie wanted to know whether her brain damage was obvious. Am I behaving like those kids in the handicapped school? Is that what everyone thinks?

My sister wasn't her chatty self. She was not somber, but pensive. Even though her sight was badly damaged for a while, her eyes sparkled with light from inside. Even some of her doctors and nurses mentioned it.

For Valerie, speaking and holding her next thought required tremendous concentration. Her verbal responses were childlike at first, and it was weeks before she could communicate very clearly. Even then her voice was raspy, and her words few. Besides her brain injury, Valerie's pain drained most of her energy.

In time she was required to sit up for forty-five minutes at a time. Each session was excruciating. In addition to broken ribs pressing her punctured lungs, her sutured diaphragm strained against her swollen organs. She had to work hard to hold her neck upright, and had to deal with the paralysis caused by strokes.

It was a long, long way from the paradise Valerie left behind.

Once she could walk from her bed to the bathroom, I helped Valerie shower a few times. She was shocked at first to see the crooked red line stretching from her upper abdomen to her navel. Clearly the doctors had rushed to save her. They needed to open her quickly and treat the organs that had been rearranged by the impact of two semis. Beauty was not on their minds. What good would a beautiful incision do if they lost the patient?

As the water ran down, Valerie traced the length of the gnarly incision with her fingers. Then she broke out in a giggle. "Where… did…I get…this?" she asked. "I don't…know where…this came from."

She seemed amused, as though trying to solve a riddle. I started to answer but was interrupted. "I don't…care," she said, "because Jesus…loves me."

Again, I started to explain.

"No," Valerie said, putting her hand on my forearm. "I mean it. He really, really loves me."

It was obvious that my sister's experience with Jesus transcended her predicament. The agony of healing was made bearable because the reality of Jesus' love consumed her. It would take some time, however, before she could articulate it.

Word by Word

Because of her strokes and brain swelling, doctors doubted Valerie would ever walk or speak again. Yet, in her second month of recovery, she was transferred to the rehab section of the hospital. She worked intensely all day, every day, and made remarkable progress.

We knew what the doctors had said. We were prepared for the worst but believed God for the best. Day by day, Valerie recovered! Her eyes cleared up and her cognition improved. Dad spent most nights in the hospital, and helped with her speech therapy. When the breathing tube was finally removed, he quizzed her with flash cards daily.

"What's this?" he asked one morning, pulling a picture from the stack. Dad knew Valerie's brain was working hard to tell her mouth what to say.

"Something you…sleep on." That was all she came up with.

"That's close," said Dad. "It begins with *ham*."

"Hammock."

"Okay!" Dad continued. "Here's another one."

She could not say the word. "It's on…a…door."

Dad encouraged her. "That's right."

"The…knob?" She was not sure.

"No. Further up the door." Dad waited. "Think about what you do with it."

Valerie had a sense of it, but the word floated by.

"It's a door knocker," Dad said without judging or adding to her frustration.

"Oh, yeah," she whispered, as though trying to imprint the information on her memory.

Valerie felt like she was in handicapped school again, but pressured this time to perform with even more challenging issues, including some blindness and a mouth numb from the strokes.

Dad continued holding up pictures. Sometimes the words came more easily than others. He remained hopeful and encouraging. The final picture that day was of an abacus. Dad did not know it, but Valerie had never been familiar with anything called an abacus. He offered a hint. "It's a way to count."

Valerie quipped, "I always…use…a…cal..cu…lator."

Dad laughed out loud.

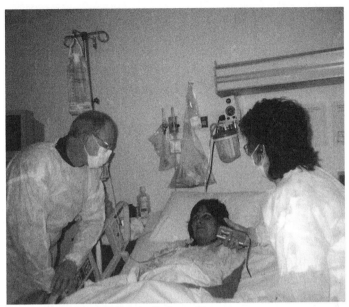

A visit from Pastor John Rusk-Mom standing by my side

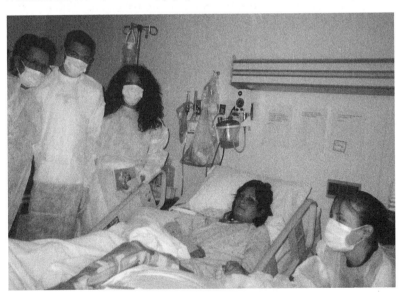

A visit from Dad, Daniel (nephew), Cheryl, and Ashley (seated)

Venturing Out

By April's end, Valerie was ready for her first appearance in the hospital corridor. Nurses were supposed to prepare her ahead of time, but when Judy arrived, her patient was dragging a full catheter bag.

"Let's have a look," she said, lifting Valerie's gown. "Oh, my gosh!" Judy exclaimed. "Her feeding tube is still attached. Her diaper needs tending!" The reprimand sent nurses scrambling.

Mom and Dad were both present, so Judy told them what to properly expect from the nursing staff. "Valerie can't navigate the halls with all this weight attached to her," Judy explained. "Before therapy, please make sure the nurses empty her catheter bag, change her diaper, and remove the feeding tube. That will be a big help to her."

It took several minutes for all the purging, redressing, and unplugging to be done. For Valerie, just existing was a full-time job. The dream of life without hoses seemed a long way off.

When the corrections were made, aides lifted Valerie back onto her feet, and Judy dressed her in a hazmat outfit: a paper dress, paper booties, and a face mask. With an oxygen tank on one side and a catheter stand on the other, Valerie was ready for battle.

With great difficulty, she put one foot in front of the other as Judy held her waist. Wearing a sneaker on her left foot and an orthopedic shoe on the right, Valerie navigated the few steps from her room to a large window at the end of the corridor.

As they ambled, Judy asked, "Do you remember what day it is, Valerie?"

"I think…it's…Thursday," Valerie whispered.

"Very good! You remembered!" Judy was elated. "And what month is it?"

Valerie was concentrating on walking and staying in one piece. I don't think she cared about what month it was. But Judy needed to know whether her patient could walk and talk at the same time.

"Remember yesterday we talked about it being a month with a major holiday when lots of people go to church?"

Valerie shuffled as she considered the question.

"It's April," offered the therapist.

"April…" Valerie mused.

It was a big moment—the first time Valerie had looked outside in more than six weeks. An entourage of staff members arrived at the window as Valerie adjusted to the bright light and the colors of spring.

"What…are…those…flowers?" she asked, pointing to a garden.

"They start with the *da* sound," prompted Judy.

"Dan…de…lions?"

"Daffodils. Aren't they beautiful?"

Valerie delighted in the loveliness of the flowers. Healing had left little time or energy for life's pleasures. Seeing the colors and the mountains surrounding Flagstaff filled her with delight.

Suddenly aware that she was tired, Valerie leaned her forehead against the warm window. Judy noticed the cue. "Are you ready to go back to your room, Valerie?"

"Please," was all Valerie could manage. Her face was flushed and the now familiar nausea returned. She was winded and perspiring, and needed to sit down.

She heard it again: "This is My Bride."

Valerie told me later how stunning the words seemed. Yet she heard them clearly, from the same voice that spoke when her spirit was sent back into her broken body. He declared again that Valerie was His beloved, even as she walked with great difficulty, dragging her catheter and wearing a diaper.

She was still His beautiful Bride.

Valerie thought, "Look at me! I'm a complete mess!"

Judy spoke, but Valerie missed it. She was so engrossed thinking about how Jesus must be laughing at the irony of it all, that she didn't remember returning to her room. But she was back in her wheelchair, having her levels checked.

"Oxygen's 96!" Judy was thrilled. "Good girl!"

Valerie's adventure had only slightly elevated her pulse. Less than two full months after the accident, she had far exceeded what doctors thought she would *ever* do again.

Valerie with therapist, Judy

9

To Each a Path

Tiny Boots (Cheryl)

For six weeks I overlooked the tiny lace-up boots beside my bedroom door. They were important, but seemed part of the landscape now, dusty and unnoticed.

On the night of the accident I was handed a bag of Valerie's belongings, which I tossed into the backseat of my car. When I returned home desperate for sleep on Tuesday night, I bathed and fell into bed, never bothering to unload the car.

Days later I opened the bag, unprepared for what I saw. My sister's clothing was shredded and bloodied. Her blouse was still damp and smelled of death, blood, and fumes. Sick to my stomach and feeling guilty, I threw the clothes out. The act might seem to indicate that she had died, but she had not died. She was *alive* and there was much to do to keep her that way.

Then I pulled out Valerie's purse...and finally, the boots. The uppers were blood-spattered. I wiped them clean with a damp rag

125

and placed the boots near the bedroom door. Sometimes when I saw them, I prayed for the day Valerie would wear them and walk in a direction she could not yet fathom.

On the day of Valerie's first walk down the hall, I spotted the boots as I prepared to go to the hospital, and held them close for a moment. "Lord, why didn't You take me through this ordeal instead of Valerie?" I prayed. "She's already been through so much."

"She has her path to walk and you have yours." I heard it and knew His voice.

Valerie had walked through the shadow of death and back again. "Bless every place she puts her feet, Lord."

It was impossible to know what that meant or where it would lead. But I couldn't help smiling. I knew the boots were made for walking, and that's what my sister would do. That's what she was already doing, one momentous step at a time.

Valerie Never Quits (Cheryl)

By the end of April, Valerie's neurologist, Dr. Brown, made an appointment with Mom and Dad. The doctor needed to explain Valerie's most recent brain x-rays. My sister Stephanie, her husband, and Pastor John accompanied Mom and Dad.

We knew that Valerie's condition was improving, but her speech was still slow. She had to work hard to make a word or idea come out right. What none of us understood was the miracle that Valerie could speak *at all*.

Dr. Brown gave a cheery "Good morning!" and pointed to images on a backlit wall. To Mom and Dad they looked like Rorschach blobs.

"Let's take a look," said Dr. Brown.

She explained, "These pictures represent layers of Valerie's brain starting from the top of her head. Imagine that your daughter is lying down on a table, and we are sitting with the top of her head directly in front of us. Each picture is a slice of her brain starting from the crown and moving toward the brain stem. Do you see that?"

Mom and Dad nodded.

"Her brain is still pretty swollen, especially on the left side where speech and language are formed. Given the swelling, it's a miracle that your daughter's speech and voluntary movement are so advanced. The speed with which she is regaining function is also miraculous."

"She's a hard worker," affirmed Dad. "She's doesn't quit."

As important as Valerie's determination was, Dr. Brown knew there was more to her progress than that. She knew we were praying, and said with a smile, "Whatever you're doing, keep doing it."

We did!

Home, Family, and a Breath of Fresh Air (Valerie)

Therapy was grueling, taking many hours each day. Some days I seemed to take one step forward and two steps back. And always, I knew that I would have to repeat the process tomorrow.

One Saturday, I felt a little blue. The routine had tired me out. Being pushed to the limit every waking hour of every day was getting old. I needed a break—maybe some sun on my face, or a shopping trip.

"Hi, Valerie!" It was Cheryl, with her camera.

Something's up.

"We came to see you!" she said in a sing-song voice.

I reached for my glasses. "What's the camera for?"

Before Cheryl could answer, Elissa walked in, dressed for her prom. Her date looked handsome but all I could see was my daughter. She was dressed in teal and her eyes were filling with tears.

"You are…beautiful," I reached out, and Elissa kissed me. It was an unforgettable moment.

"What time does prom start?" Cheryl asked from behind the camera.

"Eight o'clock," Elissa answered. "We have an hour."

I wanted to know everything: what they would do after the dance; who they were going with—*everything*. But communicating was still a struggle, so I listened instead and enjoyed one hour of feeling like a normal mother.

When everyone was gone, larger questions came to mind. Fighting to stay alive, I'd all but forgotten the struggles at home. Elissa had opted to stay with her dad, Gentry. Ashley was staying with Cheryl and Dave. I hoped the family wasn't falling apart. The thought made me feel lonely and inadequate.

Brian seemed to be coming around, though. He was truly thankful that I was alive, and he talked about God more. *Maybe I went through all this so he would know Jesus. Maybe things will be different when I get home.* Yet I knew I could not fix anything from the hospital.

Life at home would have to wait.

~

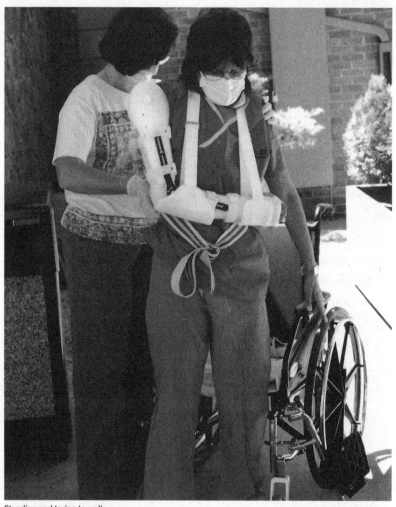

Standing and trying to walk

The next day, the nurses suggested I get some fresh air.

Really? I couldn't agree more, and could not wait to get outside! But the excursion took a long time. I had gained strength, but my gait was still slow, and I still needed to catch my breath often. A wheelchair was brought along, just in case.

In my mind, this was a test of my ability to be discharged, and I wanted to pass the test. The therapist and my mom chatted with me for the fifteen minutes it took to reach the lobby. When we reached the outside, Dad was standing in the parking lot.

"Where's the car?" asked Mom.

"Over there." Dad pointed and walked in that direction.

Am I going home? It couldn't be. But why else would my father get the car? And why did Mom seem to have a surprise up her sleeve? I eased into my wheelchair and saw Dad with a leash in his hand.

"Hoagie-bear!" I couldn't believe my eyes. My German shepherd ran toward me and sidled up cautiously. "Hoagie-bear, I...love... you!" I exclaimed. "I missed you so much, girl."

She gently bumped against my leg and panted. Was she just being careful, or was she ambivalent? My eyes stung with the confusion of it. Everyone at home was waiting for me to take my place again. Would they be ambivalent, too?

My afternoon therapy was more inspired than ever. I had been away from home too long. It was time to return to my family.

I have to get home.

Alone in the Aftermath (Ashley)

My external wounds were pretty much healed by the time Mom left the hospital at the end of May. Dad still worked long hours and couldn't provide the intensive daily care she needed. So my grandparents prepared a room for Mom to recuperate in.

When I left the hospital, I settled in with Aunt Cheryl and Uncle Dave. I wasn't sure about moving to my grandparents' home now, but I did. Everything inside me was all mixed up. I had visited Mom a couple of times, but getting to know her was hard. It was like my real mom was dead and someone I didn't know had taken her place.

This new woman needed me, as though we had switched roles. There was an aloneness that I had become accustomed to. It began in the hospital. I thought my friends would come to see me, but they didn't—at least not the ones I thought I could count on. The funny thing was that two girls from church left school at lunchtime every day to visit me. I did not expect that. I hadn't much liked going to church, and never felt that I fit in with the youth group.

I now realized it was my mom's faith that carried the two of us to church each Sunday. Yes, I was a Christian, but religion seemed to get in the way of my being honest with my mom about my questions and mistakes. It wasn't in me to be perfect. By nature I wanted to test boundaries. But Church tested me. It kept me bumping up against what was right and what was wrong.

Besides, I wondered how my Mom's faith helped her. Didn't she almost die in the wreck? And wasn't she doing badly afterward? Practically speaking, the accident took her away from me forever. I had no real relationship with Dad. Elissa was working. Even when I was thrown into that triangle of pavement, I was all by myself. Alone.

That is where I'd been ever since. Dave Dobbs, the firefighter, said it was a miracle. He said the angels put me there. But how could I square the love and protection of God with the catastrophe we suffered?

I asked God some serious questions. *Nothing was perfect before the wreck, anyway. Why did You have to make it worse? What kind of God are You?* Even asking seemed to isolate me from the answer. Those days in the hospital with everyone focused on Mom gave me plenty of time to put up walls. No Mother. No God I could relate to. No answers to my questions. Without realizing it, I had moved away from discovering what I needed most— His love.

This was the daughter my mom came home to.

10

MEMORIES AND MIRACLES

Talking Heaven, on the Sofa (Cheryl)

Immediately following Valerie's release from the hospital, setting a routine was a priority. There was plenty to do. More rehab was still ahead, and rest was important. But other details needed attention, too.

Late in that first week I took my sister to the mall to buy tennis shoes. It was just Valerie and me—our first outing in months. It would take a while to get to the shoe store, because we stopped first at H&R Block. Our excited coworkers surrounded Valerie. I was worried that it might be too much for her, but she enjoyed it so much that we visited her friends in other stores, too.

After the mall, we returned to an empty house and spent some sister time together. Seeing Valerie seated on the sofa was so special. I was struck by the normalcy of it. *Oh, dear God. She made it.* I sat beside her, not realizing until that moment how tired I was.

135

Cheryl and Valerie (November 2013)

Finally, we could look into each other's eyes and acknowledge the hellish thing we'd been through. And finally, we could take a victory lap. All this time, we had worked to keep it all together. Now we could let go, if only for a moment.

And let go we did. The tears flowed until we could barely see one another. "I'm sorry," I sniffed. "I missed you so much." I kissed Valerie's face and brushed back a lock of her hair.

"I missed you, too." Valerie was weary, too, and relieved to be home. And she had questions to ask. Some had been put on hold, for fear of the answers. Now she looked me in the face and asked, "What...what happened...in the...accident...to Ashley?"

"She was thrown from the car, Valerie." It took time for her to process information, so I didn't know how much to say all at once.

"Her injuries. What were…her injuries, Cheryl?" She set her jaw and braced for the answer.

"Fractured bones, chipped teeth, lacerated tongue, cracked pelvis, ruptured bladder…"

Valerie covered her face with her left hand and wept. She hadn't been there for her baby. She hadn't known how bad it was.

"She's doing well, Valerie. Don't cry." I patted her back. "I know it hurts that she hasn't seen you more. It's been hard for her."

Valerie composed herself and asked, "How long…was she in the…hospital?"

"Nine days." I wiped my wet face with my hands. "It was a miracle, you know."

"In what way?"

"Ashley was thrown into an empty space created when the big rigs folded into each other." I formed the shape with my hands to illustrate. "The firemen called it the miracle triangle. The angels must have put her there. It was the only place she could've landed without being hit by other vehicles in the pileup."

"So…God took…care…of her there." Valerie understood: God had always known that they would be all right.

"He took care of you, too, Valerie. If Ashley had not been ejected, you both would have died. Instead, you fell sideways into her empty seat. God saved both of you."

I knew Valerie was piecing together the memories, picturing the hours pinned beneath the semi. It was hard to go there. But something beautiful came out of the horror: unforgettable memories of Him.

"You know, Cheryl...I saw...Jesus." Valerie paused to catch her breath. "In heaven."

"I know." *Here it is! I've waited months for this moment.* "God took me there, Valerie. I saw you."

Valerie's eyes widened. "What...did...you see?"

"You were in a river."

"Swimming with...Jesus," Valerie continued.

"Yes!" My laughter pealed. What a joy it was to remember it—what a relief to finally share it. "Do you remember, Valerie?"

"He splashed...water...on me."

"I know what you were wearing." I waited for Valerie to say it. She waited to see if I got it right.

"What was I wearing?"

"A sheer purple gown, like a tunic or robe."

Valerie inhaled sharply. "Yes! I was!"

"You said, 'Taste and see that the Lord is good.' You laughed and threw water on me."

Valerie did not remember my being there. "I did?"

"What was He like, Valerie?" I moved so she could look straight at me. "Jesus. What was He like?"

"Light," she began. "He looks like light. I wish you could understand... the way I did in heaven, Cheryl." Valerie paused and seemed far away. "I wish I didn't have...to use words. Because they...can't possibly... describe the beauty...His face...His eyes...the fire behind them... the way it made...their blue-green color...electric."

Valerie's speech was still halting, but she was animated. "And He hums, Cheryl. His body...hums. Like...electricity...power coming from Him." Thoughts came faster than she could process. "I couldn't look...straight at Him. His face was...so bright. Like a flash...from a camera." She laughed then. "I think...that's what's wrong...with my eyes now...seeing that brilliance."

"What was heaven like?" I was rapt with anticipation.

"At first...it was light...and noise. But then...I turned around... and He was...coming...toward me. Jesus. He held...out His arms. Then He said, 'Valerie, don't you ...know how much...I love you?'"

Valerie was seeing the scene again. She seemed to ache with the yearning for Him. She sobbed and said, "Jesus spoke…my name… Cheryl." Trying to compose herself, she said, "He loves…*me*."

The story began to make perfect sense. For weeks Valerie had been saying that Jesus loves her. His open arms, His declarations of love, her being bathed in the light of His presence—these experiences traveled back to Earth with my sister and drove her recovery. That was the fragrance the nurses mentioned. It explained the peace surrounding her, the serene way that she handled adversity, and her swift, inexplicable recovery.

Valerie was changed. She walked above the storms she once lived in. Life here had not changed all that much, but her understanding of another life transformed Valerie.

Knowing it would touch a sore spot, I offered my confession. "I had to call you back to us, Valerie. Jesus told me to pray you back."

Her body slouched. She looked dejected. "I didn't…want to… come back, Cheryl."

"I know. That might be why Jesus let me see you in the river. He wanted me to know what coming back would cost you."

"You can't…imagine." Valerie cried softly. "I am…so…homesick."

It was our first talk about heaven. There would be many more, but it would be awhile before Valerie could share her sweetest memories. When that time came, she told me how she wished she could press her heart against mine and transfer the entire experience, without words.

Words would never do. They could not.

Only God (Valerie)

A Surprise in the Heap

A friend of mine had seen my Jeep in a storage yard. I wanted to see it, too. Maybe it would help me understand everyone's amazement at my survival. Could it have been that bad? Because litigation was pending, lawyers had the car safely stored. One Saturday I asked Brian, "Can we go see the car today?"

"It's pretty torn up, Valerie. You probably won't recognize it as a car, much less your Jeep."

"That's okay," I replied. "I still want to see it."

"Okay. Let's go." Brian figured I deserved to see what was left of the car I almost died in.

The wrecking yard manager led us to something hidden under a giant blue tarp. As he and Brian peeled away the cover, I was astounded to think it was an automobile. Its rear end was wrapped around toward the passenger door. The back seat was gone. The whole thing looked like a child had cut it to shreds with a giant pair of scissors.

I looked into the tiny "coffin" that once trapped me. *How did I live through that? How did I fit in such a tiny space? No wonder my body was crushed!* The logistics were unimaginable. Then I thought of something else.

"Brian, I think my Bible's in there somewhere."

He was bewildered. "I don't know how in the world I can get to it."

But he tried. There were many sharp edges to get past before he could find the console—if the console even existed.

"Brian, be careful," I warned.

"I'm going to find it for you, Valerie." He was determined, even cutting his hands and arms in the search.

Bloodied and victorious, he retrieved my Bible! "Here it is!"

I took the precious book from Brian's bleeding hand, and sobbed. Like me, my Bible had a puncture wound in its center. And like me, it had survived. I felt for the sewn-up hole in my abdomen, still puckered and knotty. Yes, we were both wounded. But we were still standing.

He was wounded for our transgressions. He was bruised for our iniquities. The chastisement of our peace is upon Him. And by His stripes we are healed. All the way home, these verses from Isaiah 53 flowed from my heart to my head and back again.

It was another miracle: my Bible and I made it out, mostly in one piece.

Valerie's first time seeing her car since the accident, and finding her Bible inside

The Testimony and the Cross

Late that summer a reporter named Sean Johnson asked to write an article about my recovery. He wrote for the Christian paper, *The Summit,* and was intrigued by the story of my rescue, and my experiences in heaven. When we met, he photographed me on the front lawn of Flagstaff Medical Center.

"What do you remember of the accident?" Sean asked.

"I remember saying, 'Jesus, help me,' and I remember crying."

"Did you think you would die?" he continued.

"When they took me out of the car, my body went limp. I'd used all my energy to stay alive. I remembered the story about Moses and Aaron as they stood between the living and the dead. That's where I felt like I was."

The interview was the first of many. This one, however, brought a miracle of its own. The photo included in the story showed a cross displayed prominently on the plate glass window behind me.

"There's no cross there," Cheryl said when she saw the article. "I was at that hospital a hundred times."

"There's not," I agreed. "The reporter even said so in the paper. See?"

There it was. A disclaimer: "The cross in the upper left of the photo was not planned or superimposed."[1]

"I'm going to the hospital to look," said Cheryl.

There was no cross inside or outside of the hospital. There was no cross anywhere in the landscape around the building—nothing that could have been reflected in the window. Yet a cross appeared in the photo.

Valerie outside hospital; cross appears in upper left (not superimposed).[2]

Mounting the Hurdles

There were many encouragements like this along the way, but there were many frustrations, too. Rehabilitation was a slow process. At times, I was tempted to quit. One morning, still struggling to use my blow dryer, I dropped it onto the counter.

"My body won't work for me, Jesus!" I declared, exasperated.

"My Body won't work for Me, either," I heard Him say. It was a clear reference to the Church. In John 17, Jesus prayed for His Body to be unified. Yet, two thousand years later, the Church is fragmented.

My frustration still festered. When Cheryl came over later that day, I challenged her. "Why did you pray me back here?"

"Valerie, if you have a problem with that, you need to take it up with Jesus."

Long hours on her face in the hospital chapel must have flashed in Cheryl's mind. She probably struggled with the weight of those prayers even now. "He's the one who told me to pray that way."

Cheryl's answer was dead serious. So was my question. Coming back was hard. So many things were wrong. My body rejected food at first. After not eating for weeks, my digestive system was lazy. My appetite was almost nonexistent. I wanted to eat, but all I could do with food was stare at it.

Wondering what might seem appetizing to me, Brian asked, "What would you like to eat?"

"A fish fillet with extra sauce," I said.

It sounded good when I said it, but eating it was another story. I barely managed two bites. I did, however, get tartar sauce all over the paralyzed side of my mouth.

Not until January 2001 did I feel comfortable enough with eating to have lunch with the intercessory prayer group. My right hand was numb and crooked. Eating a sandwich was messy. When I finally got it into my mouth, I bit down on a hard, unidentified object. Quickly, I yanked out the sandwich. With all eyes on me, I laughed hysterically.

I had bitten down on my numb finger!

One thing still worked—*faith*. It kept me moving forward. That meant getting up and doing things even when nothing worked right. A question from Jesus put the situation in perspective for me. He asked, "What will you do with the circumstances you have?"

I replied with a question: "How do You want me to do this?"

Some days it seemed like too much. Yet I understood that I needed to tell my body, soul, and spirit what to do. And they *had to do it.* I spoke to my hand. "You will work," I said. Then I put demands on my body, graduating from the easier treadmill to the more complex elliptical machine: "You were designed to work, body, so do it."

It took months for the nerve damage to improve. The frustration of speaking was often so great that I became angry. Dr. Tim Martin suggested hyperbaric oxygen therapy to hasten the repair of my damaged brain cells.

"Your brain has some 'sleeping beauties,' Valerie," said Dr. Martin.

"Well, wake them up!" I quipped.

He laughed. "That's exactly what we're going to do—energize them with some pressurized oxygen. They are too tired to do much of anything right now. I'll bet you are experiencing some fatigue and irritability, right?"

"Yes." I smiled. "I hope you're saying that it's from brain damage and not a bad personality."

"That's exactly what I'm saying," he laughed.

The hyperbaric treatments were enjoyable. With several other people, I entered what looked like a submarine. Oxygen flowed through a tube in my nose, but some patients wore full face masks. For ninety minutes we relaxed and watched movies as we inhaled healing doses of oxygen. The results were immediate and amazing. My speech kicked into gear and my thought processes became clearer. Even my energy for life returned.

Dr. Martin suggested that we try one other therapy. "I know vision is still an issue, so let's see if we can wake up your thalamus with Eyelights."

"*Eyelights?*" I asked. "I've never heard of them."

"They're special glasses. They'll make you look pretty cool, too. They produce a blinking light that sends rays through the nondominant eye to the thalamus. Because of your strokes, one of your eyes is more active than the other. So, the visual cues that should help answer questions like *where, how,* and *what* aren't helping as much as they should."

"I still have trouble with pictures, too," I confessed.

"Yes. Because still images and even colors, aren't registering with your brain properly."

"Then let's light up my eyes."

The neurologist could tell his patient understood. And I was thankful for whatever progress we might make.

Valerie with Dr Timothy Martin (May 2014)

Notes

1. Sean Johnson, "A miracle of survival and salvation," The Summit, Vol. 3, No. 3, July–September 2000.

2. Photo by Sean Johnson for his article, "A miracle of survival and salvation."

11

NEW HORIZONS

The New Normal (Ashley)

It was nearly Christmas in the year 2000 when Mom and I returned to our house. It was a milestone, but there were many unknowns. I was at my grandparents' house while Mom continued her rehabilitation, but I did not handle her care. Now that she was home, I wondered what life would be like.

On the first night, our whole family came over to celebrate. The next night, church and neighborhood friends began bringing us evening meals. We were back in our normal setting, but it was a confusing chapter of my life. Even with just Mom, Dad, Elissa, and me at the table, I was uncomfortable. "How do we do this?" I kept wondering, "How do we carry on like this is normal?"

Mom regained function daily, but I also sensed the difference *in her.* There was a new gentleness, and an inexplicable distance that I could not figure out. Which one of us had moved, and what did it mean?

The new normal also meant that I had to grow up and be a mother to my mother—at fourteen. There were many things she still could not do for herself, and many new things I had to learn about her and about my emotions. My loneliness did not end just because our family was together again. Somehow, I needed to make my mom *mine* again. I'd already lost her once. I could not bear to lose her again.

Still, Mom's experience in heaven and the changes it made in her breathed new life into my faith. Day by day, a flame was sparked inside me. Today I can confidently say that it is possible to go through terrible things, and move on. I have learned that lesson by experience. I have made some great choices since then, and some real mistakes. But now I know that I'm never alone.

Jesus isn't just my mother's God anymore. I have made Him mine, too. I know He answers my prayers, because He's there when I call. Best of all, He loves me whether or not I'm perfect.

One day I'll see Him face to face and He will say, "Ashley, don't you know how much I love you?"

Ashley and Valerie at the park (November 2012)

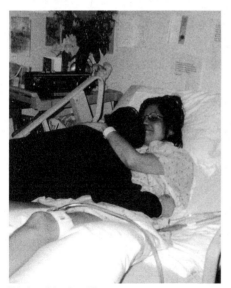

Valerie and daughter, Elissa

The Disneyland Parable (Valerie)

Months after I left the hospital I shared something new with Cheryl. "You know," I said, "people always ask me what heaven is like. I've been thinking about how to share the experience in a way they can visualize."

"You mean like Jesus did in the parables?" she asked.

"Exactly. Jesus always explained the kingdom of heaven in terms of earthly things—a pearl of great price, a vineyard, a man sowing seeds. I think I can compare heaven to Disneyland."

Cheryl was perplexed. "Okay. Tell me how."

"Well, first of all there's the anticipation. You know, driving into the parking lot everybody's happy and rushing to the trams. Then as we near the gates, we hear the music playing. We can peek in and see everyone taking pictures by the Mickey Mouse landscape."

"Well, it is the happiest place on Earth." Cheryl grinned.

"When you walk through the gates, there are different places to choose, like Adventureland, Frontierland, and Tomorrowland." I knew I was reaching, but the comparison made sense. "Cheryl, when I was in heaven I walked through the gates into a land of restoration, the oasis where Jesus restored my heart. But there were other places, too."

"I remember you telling me about landscapes that looked like the four seasons at their peak. You saw them from the mountain where Jesus took you."

I could tell Cheryl was getting excited, so I continued. "Of course, when I was there, I didn't think, 'Oh, this is like Disneyland.' But I want people to have a vision of how it might feel. The happiest place on Earth is no match for the happiest place *anywhere!*"

"How else are heaven and Disneyland alike?" Cheryl asked.

"At Disneyland, the atmosphere is charged. We become like children again, anticipating the attractions and waiting to be amazed. Heaven's atmosphere is charged in a different way, but it still made me giggly. I was so joyful I couldn't contain it! And just like at Disneyland, there were so many choices. Heaven is like that, but more so. It's too much to take in all at once."

Words are never enough to describe heaven, because Jesus is what makes heaven, *heaven*. It is one of a kind. Disney is not heaven. In heaven, I wasn't just part of a crowd. I was Valerie, His beloved.

"Remember when we went to the 3-D movie at Disneyland where the dad shrunk his kids?" I asked Cheryl. "Remember how the characters came right up to your face like they were popping out of the screen?"

"Yes! I always flinched! Like it was personal!" Cheryl laughed.

"That's my point. It's 3-D. It singles you out and gets right in your face. But it gets in other peoples' faces, too! Everyone experiences the same thing at the same time!"

"And how is that like heaven?" Cheryl asked.

"While Jesus was so focused on me, He interacted with everyone else who entered heaven. He is extremely personal, yet He cannot be contained. While I was there, I felt like I had Him all to myself. But every other soul received love and attention from Him, too— and at the same time."

Suddenly I was missing Him again. How I wanted to see His face looking into mine.

Cheryl saw it. "You're homesick, Valerie. I can tell."

"I wish I could take you there," I said, blinking back my tears. "I wish I could adequately tell you what He's like."

Then it gelled in my mind: Jesus was fierce, untamed, like a lion not to be tangled with. He could have annihilated everyone and everything. I felt that. I understood the humming to be His restrained omnipotence. But at the same time, He was tender. He wrapped me in love and protected me. I knew that the wrath He was capable of expressing would never be turned on me.

"Jesus is fiery, Cheryl. I knew at once that He is innocent, yet strong; passionate but not overbearing. It was like looking into a diamond or prism. Different aspects of Him sparkled all at once."

I gathered my thoughts. "It's hard to describe the mighty God."

"Valerie, if everyone was as sure about going to heaven as you are, death would not make them fearful. Everyone would anticipate it the way kids look forward to Disneyland."

"I wish I could go to heaven now, Cheryl."

Valerie and Aleia Meet…Again (Cheryl)

It was March 11, 2002, two years after the accident—a banner day. My daughter Shannon had just given birth, and Dave and I rejoiced over our first grandchild, Aleia.

When Valerie and I walked to the hospital nursery, the nurses put Aleia near the glass so we could see her. Valerie caught her breath. The baby looked straight into her eyes. Every time Valerie moved, the newborn's eyes followed her.

"She's watching you, Valerie. Move over there. Look! She watches you wherever you go!"

"I've seen her before." Valerie whispered and grabbed my arm. "I saw her in heaven." The memory was still fresh. "When I first saw Jesus, Grandpa Isaac was there, too. I knew who he was although he was much younger, maybe in his forties. We didn't speak, but I knew he was enjoying my encounter with Jesus."

I listened, awestruck.

"There were two little girls. Aleia was one of them. It's her eyes, Cheryl. She seemed to be about three years old, but I recognize those eyes." Valerie stared at Aleia. "I wonder who the other child was."

All that day, Valerie soaked in the fresh sense of heaven. She was still homesick, and still in love.

My sister was with me when Aleia came home. "Come on, Valerie. You have to feel this little bundle in your arms."

Valerie shook her head. "I'm afraid to, Cheryl." "My right arm is weak. I might drop her."

"No you won't." I plopped the swaddled child into my sister's lap.

Valerie was still mesmerized by Aleia's eyes. There was a kinship as she spoke. "Do you remember me? Don't forget where you came from."

Aleia seemed fascinated with Valerie, too. Even after I handed her back to Shannon, Aleia looked across the room for Valerie.

Aleia is now twelve, and her adoring great aunt still reminds her where she came from. And the other child? Her name is Ariel. She is Valerie's granddaughter, Elissa's child.

∾

In 2001, around the time Flagstaff therapists reported having done all they could for Valerie, Dave and I moved to Phoenix.

Dr. Martin also relocated there. The changes seemed to be the prompting Valerie needed. Brian didn't want to relocate, but the promise of better care for Valerie sealed the deal. And Dr. Martin would continue working with her.

Phoenix was a good move. There, Valerie came more fully into her healing, both mentally and physically.

Jerusalem and Jesus' Eyes

In December 2002, Valerie, Cheryl, and Ashley signed up for Benny Hinn's Israel tour. Valerie was still moving slowly and wearing her Eyelights. Her brain was processing better but, she was not yet ready for a national speaking tour.

Five hundred other pilgrims made the trip, among them Aaron Gowens, a gregarious pastor from South Carolina. After watching and wondering for two whole days, he asked Valerie, "What is up with those blinking glasses?"

"I saw Jesus and it blinded me."

"You for real?" Aaron asked. "Are you telling me you actually saw Jesus?"

"She did," added Cheryl. "You should hear her story."

"I was in a car accident two years ago. I went to heaven while my body was in intensive care."

Valerie yearned to tell this man about the Jesus she met, and Aaron wanted to hear every detail. By the time they parted ways, he had arranged for the sisters to testify before his congregation. The invitation was daunting. They said they would pray about it.

Much of the Israel trip was physically challenging for Valerie. Yet she was determined to make it up every staircase and down each street. Tsvika, the tour guide was awed by Valerie's perseverance. So was everyone else on the bus.

Security guards were also assigned to the buses. A young Israeli soldier named Eldad rode with Valerie and Cheryl's group. One day when Valerie looked down the steep incline of a certain tourist site, she was dubious about whether she could make it back up the steps.

Eldad made a proposition. "I'm very, very strong. If you want to go down, I will carry you back up."

"It's a deal."

Taking Cheryl's arm, Valerie started the descent. She lagged behind the group, but never gave up. "You have to keep your promise, Eldad!"

He laughed. "You made it all this way just so I'd have to prove that I could carry you up?"

Proud to be chivalrous, Eldad hoisted Valerie onto his back and ran up the steep steps. Everyone cheered as my sister and her knight made it to the top.

"You are Wonder Woman!" the tour guide exclaimed as Valerie boarded the bus.

The moniker stuck. For the remainder of the trip, Valerie was known as Wonder Woman.

~

One day was set aside for a trip to Mahane Yhuda Market. The place was crammed with people and local produce. Rugs hung from kiosks beside a stack of flatbread pizzas. Mothers with strollers and dads carrying children on their shoulders watched as minstrels sang. It was a colorful scene.

Valerie and Cheryl slowly made their way through the labyrinth and paused beneath the awning of a small bakery. "Maybe we can get something to drink here," Cheryl said.

As Cheryl searched for bottled water, Valerie watched people playing backgammon and sipping minted beverages. Cheryl soon returned, but without water.

"The lines were too long. Let's walk a little further," she said. "Maybe we'll find some water there."

In the midst of the crowd, Valerie felt someone close against her. There were people pressing from every direction, yet Valerie turned to look. A man's face was up against hers. She was electrified by what she saw, and stopped so abruptly that the man almost knocked her down.

Jesus. The yearning for her lost love combined with intense homesickness. *I want to see His face again…to touch it and hear Him say He loves me. I want to go home.*

"Valerie, what's the matter?" Cheryl asked.

"That man's eyes."

"What man?" *There are several hundred men!*

It was too late; the crowd had swallowed him. Valerie knew he was not her Jesus, yet she wanted to run after him. "Cheryl, his eyes were the exact color of Jesus' eyes."

"Made you homesick, huh?"

"Oh…you have no idea."

~

The next day, the group headed back to the States. Pastor Aaron had already arranged for the sisters to fly to South Carolina. The friendship also fueled a second Israel trip, this one arranged by Cheryl. In 2005, they planned to meet Pastor Gowens in Tel Aviv.

"Hey, Valerie, guess who our tour guide is?" Cheryl's enthusiasm bubbled over.

"I'm guessing Tsvika since I don't know any other Israeli tour guides," Valerie replied, laughing.

"You're right!"

Tsvika couldn't believe it was the same Valerie. "You look so strong!" he said as they rode the tram to the ancient fortress, Masada. Tsvika pointed to a trail and said, "The next time you come we'll hike to the top!"

"Okay, Tsvika!" laughed Valerie. "Next time."

During the trip, Aaron taped another interview with Valerie. This time she was able to articulate her experience so clearly that he aired the interview on the TV station that carried his sermons. More than two million people watched it!

Valerie left Israel feeling more ready to share her experiences publicly. People began asking when she would write a book. She prayed for God's timing. It did not take long for Him to open the door.

Eldad carrying Valerie up the stairs (Israel, 2002)

A Surprise in the Philippines

In 2008, the sisters were attending Church for the Nations in Phoenix and decided to take a missions trip to the Philippines. They landed in Manila having no idea that Valerie was about to share her story with five million people.

The itinerary included a trip to Davao City where Amy Muranko headed Global Impact Ministries. The young American was staying at the ministry residence when she met Cheryl and Valerie, who casually shared their story of heaven. Amy was so moved that she contacted a television station. Immediately, the sisters were invited to appear with Amy on a Christian show called *Kapihan uban ni Dottie.*[1]

The program began with worship. Like the studio, the worship was simple. The sisters were caught up in the sincerity of it. Valerie was also comforted by the worship, and by knowing that she and Cheryl would appear on the air together.

After worship, the show's host, Dottie Abrina, took charge, saying, "Thank the Lord! Thank the Lord!"

Then Dottie sang a song and introduced her guests. "We have a guest today who the enemy wanted to kill. But the Lord wouldn't allow it."

After a minor video malfunction, the audience watched as Scott McGee from Channel 3 in Flagstaff reported on the wreck. There were pictures of the crash scene and an interview with Bob Hiser, the fire captain.

When the video ended, Dottie made what had become her signature statement: "This is the day that the Lord has made, let us rejoice and be glad in it!"² She turned to Amy and thanked her for coming.

"Thank you, Dottie, for having me co-host today."

"So, Aim," Dottie said with a familiarity Amy seemed to embrace, "I saw the video clippings and saw that Valerie is in heaven."

"Well, she went to heaven," Amy explained. "But she came back."

Valerie was then escorted to the set. Dottie observed, "You are here. Back from heaven."

Valerie's shyness returned. So did the excitement of sharing her story.

Amy stepped in. "I've had the privilege of hearing this story," she said. "Valerie, can you tell us what you remember of the accident?"

This was always the difficult part of the story. "I woke up trapped in my car, beneath a big rig. I was in a room by myself. I knew I was dying."

Dottie asked. "So did you die right away?"

"Two hours—"

Dottie interrupted. "After two hours you were pronounced dead."

Valerie's thoughts still moved more slowly than she liked. "They didn't pronounce me dead because they wanted to harvest my organs...wanted them fresh for donation. So they kept me alive."

Amy explained how life support is used to keep donor organs viable. Then she suggested getting Cheryl's side of the story.

As Cheryl joined them on the set, Dottie welcomed her. "Tell us more about the accident."

Cheryl began the difficult account from her perspective. "There was a pileup on a snowy highway when Valerie stopped in the far right lane beside a large big rig parked on the shoulder. Another semi rammed into the back of Valerie's car. That's when Ashley was ejected and thrown to the pavement...a small triangle of the highway hidden away, sheltered by the Lord. A second truck hit the first truck, forcing Valerie's car completely beneath the parked semi. If Ashley hadn't been in that little triangle she would've been hit by other cars that were smashing into each other in the snow."

"When did you hear about the accident?" Dottie asked.

"Dave, a firefighter who also went to our church, was on scene. God showed him the Jeep hood ornament and a cassette tape of a sermon from our church. He put two and two together and called his wife."

Amy looked at Valerie. "Valerie, tell us about going to heaven."

Valerie was excited to share. "When I crossed over, I took a deep breath, and there was no pain. I didn't have lungs, though. It was something different. When I turned around, I saw Jesus and ran up to Him to touch His face. 'It's You. It's really You!' I kept repeating. Then I fell into Him and realized He never draws back. I was inside Him then. Like Jesus prayed in John 17 right before His death: 'May they all be one, just as You, Father, are in Me, and I in You, that they may also be in us.' I realized that the Bible is literal. That total intimacy. Jesus consumed me and I consumed Him. I was giggly…inside."

Valerie remembered the ecstasy. "You know when you're tickled here on Earth, you can't take it for very long. But there I felt giggly all the time."

Dottie wanted to know whether Jesus took Valerie to different places in heaven. But Valerie wasn't finished with the most important part—the love story. "The first thing Jesus said was, 'Valerie, don't you know how much I love you?'"

Valerie was caught up again. "He knew my name. He opened His arms to embrace me. Iridescence was so thick in the air that it moved along with His arms. Time stood still. I didn't know He knew my name."

A knot in her throat made Valerie pause. "I had all kinds of issues before the accident."

Amy listened closely. "Tell us about that, Valerie."

"I had lots of surgeries on my feet between the ages of seven and eleven—a generational disease that affects the muscles. It's called familial muscular dystrophy. Before each operation, my parents took me to the elders to be prayed over, but nothing happened. I wasn't healed. I really believe God does miracles, but He didn't for me. I even went to an Oral Roberts tent meeting where it seemed to me that everyone else got healed *except me*."

Valerie looked down. "I figured I wasn't good enough for God to heal me. The neighborhood kids called me a 'retard' because I had to go to a handicapped school. When you grow up hearing those things, you feel you don't quite measure up. You know—self-hatred. It's a mindset."

Valerie continued. "When Jesus said He loves me, the words were so exciting because He changed that mindset. I am lovable and worthy of His attention. Jesus touched my head and from His hands came an ointment, rich and gleaming like honey. It flowed down my body, and when it hit the ground in front of my feet I knew that I knew that I knew Jesus loved me."

Valerie closed her eyes momentarily. "When I saw how He felt about me...when I saw what He saw...that Jesus thought I was beautiful...I never thought that. I always felt guilt and condemnation."

Amy understood. Life informs us incorrectly sometimes. "I think we grow up in life and get perceptions of things. Because we live in a sinful world, we get belief systems that don't line up with God's thoughts about us. Valerie had mindsets that she believed. God took those belief systems and blasted them out of her mind. Then He put truth directly into her."

"Did you feel guilty while you were there?" Dottie asked.

"Oh, no!" Valerie giggled. "I felt totally clean. I was perfect. He made me like Him."

"Where did you go after He poured the honey over you?"

"To a river where Jesus splashed me." *It's always fun to tell this part.*

Amy was floored. "You mean Jesus splashed you?"

Laughing, Valerie smiled. "Yes. He did!"

"All the kids out there are going to be excited to hear that Jesus is fun," said Amy looking straight through the camera at those kids.

"We had a good time," replied Valerie. "He makes even the serious things seem fun."

"So, He likes to have fun and laugh?" Amy asked.

"That's all we did," remembered Valerie. "Joy unspeakable and full of glory.[3] What you read is really more than you can imagine. And I saw my daughters there."

"Really?" Amy was astonished. "But aren't they still alive?"

"Yes," affirmed Valerie. "However, in heaven they were sitting at a table with many others. I wasn't a participant, though...more of an onlooker."

"That should be encouraging to those parents who are praying for their children and grandchildren," Amy noted.

Dottie chimed in. "God isn't on a timeline, is He? He sees from the beginning to the end. It makes perfect sense that God looks at the past and the future all at once. He let you see that with Him!"

"I saw my grandchildren, too." Valerie added. "They were not yet born at the time. And I saw my great-niece standing with my grandfather, Isaac!"

"Isaac means laughter." Amy smiled at the thought.

"Yes, and my grandfather was smiling at me. He'd already passed, but I knew it was Grandpa."

"How tall is Jesus?" Dottie asked.

Okay. I've never been asked that or even thought about it. "Over six feet, I would guess. But, you know, Dottie, He's spirit and light. His eyes are like fire. Jesus is passionate for us."

"Did Jesus tell you He would send you back? Because I bet you didn't like Jesus to send you back."

"He told me He wanted me to go back. That was the will of Jesus for me. But, of course, I wanted to stay with Him. Jesus kept talking to me, though." *The same way He kept asking me if I would die for Him. A persistent addressing of His will. I've never put that together with heaven before.*

"I finally said, 'Lord, I'll do whatever You want me to do. But I'd rather stay with You.' We went to a small room that reminds me of a birthing room…the massage room at a spa… dim lighting…a small bed. I lay down and fell into a deep sleep."

"It's awesome that you said you'd do His will, Valerie," Amy interjected. "He asked you, didn't He? Jesus didn't force you. Do you notice that's the same way He treats us on Earth?"

Remembering her earlier thought, Valerie replied, "Yes, Jesus talks until we change our minds." She smiled, remembering His countenance.

"Why did He send you back?" Amy asked intently. "What does Jesus want you to do here on Earth?"

"To tell people that He loves them…" Valerie began.

Exuberant, Dottie cut her off. "And that there is heaven. Some people think there's no heaven." Dottie looked into Amy's eyes. "Aim, there are people who think heaven's here on the Earth!"

"How can Dottie's viewers be assured they will be in heaven after they die?" asked Amy.

"They ask Jesus into their hearts." Valerie recognized the importance of the question. "Jesus is real. Heaven is real. God loves us. This Earth is a testing ground. It's an illusion. For me, the curtain was pulled back and I saw reality. Whose report will we believe? What we see or what God tells us? After the accident, my body didn't respond very well. Since then Jesus has been teaching me about believing God's report. The doctors said that if I lived, I'd be a vegetable. Well, I'd say I'm a pretty lively vegetable!"

"So Jesus let Valerie get into an accident to reveal that He loves her. Because you didn't believe that before?" Dottie tried connecting the dots. "You were a Christian before?"

Amy cut in. "She knew intellectually, but it wasn't truth down deep in her heart."

Dottie had a point to make. "People are deceived by thinking that they aren't special. Even people in this audience don't believe Jesus loves them." Dottie spoke earnestly. "You don't have to die to know that. Now you can be convinced in Jesus' name!"

"That's the point of the entire interview, isn't it?" added Amy. "That Jesus loves you so very much."

Dottie wanted Cheryl's takeaway. "What do you know now that you didn't before?"

"That nothing is impossible with God. Prayer is important and changes things. I prayed for a child who died. I interceded, yearning for his healing. Not long afterward, another intercessor told me that, because of my faith, I would see the dead raised. Valerie is the answer to that."

"So when will you write the book?" Amy asked.

"When we find that person," Cheryl said. "We are praying about it all the time."

In the final minutes of the interview, Dottie turned to Valerie. "This broadcast will be all over the world today. In real time, over five million people watched as you shared your experience with heaven."

"We didn't want to tell you that before the show," said Amy, giggling. "We didn't want to make you too nervous."

The studio lights dimmed. Cheryl and Valerie walked to the waiting van. It occurred to them that, in His sovereignty, Jesus was arranging opportunities to talk about Valerie's heavenly journey.

"I always wonder what's next," Valerie said.

"Me, too, Valerie. Me, too."

Notes

1. Interview excerpts are from Dottie Abrina's program, Kapihan uban ni Dottie, on DCBC (Davao Christian Bible Channel), October 2008. (Some excerpts have been paraphrased.)
2. See Psalms 118:24.
3. See First Peter 1:8.

Cheryl and Valerie arrive in the Philippines.

12

His Purposes, His Bride

Dream and Fulfillment (Cheryl)

On May 1, 2003 I awoke from a dream, and wrote in my prayer journal: I don't know if this is from the Lord, but I have a sense in my spirit that it is. I'll see what God does to bring us together.

All I knew about the woman in the dream was that her last name was Carter and I'd seen her on Christian television. In the dream, she saw me interceding, and began pacing and interceding herself. She picked up a white sheet and covered both of us with it. Underneath the sheet, we prayed together.

On September 11, 2008, the dream came to pass when I threw a party for Valerie's birthday and invited friends from the intercessory prayer group. One of them had met Pamela Carter at a media conference. Confident that Pamela would want to hear Valerie's story of heaven, she invited her to the party.

As the women helped themselves to refreshments, the conversation turned to heaven and Valerie's adventure there. Pamela was intrigued. She was in the process of creating a film about heaven and hell at the time.

"I've been praying for months," she said, "asking the Lord to give me a team of intercessors for this project."

Oh my gosh!

"Just a minute," I said, pushing back my chair. "I'll be right back."

When I returned, I opened my prayer journal to May 1, 2003, and read aloud the account of my dream.

"That is such confirmation!" Pamela said, grinning from ear to ear. "You might just be my answered prayer."

After dinner the group prayed about Pamela's project and pledged to continue praying. And, as a result of our meeting, Pamela interviewed Valerie and me on her program through XP Media. Pamela's exchange with Valerie revealed the poignancy of her encounter with Christ.

The Interview[1]

Pamela Carter introduced Valerie with a biblical reference: "With us today is Valerie Paters, who has her very own Lazarus story of coming back from the dead. Although, she wasn't really dead because she was with Jesus. Whether you say dead or alive, in and out of consciousness…what we know is that Valerie was with Jesus for at least three days while her body languished in the intensive care area of Flagstaff Medical Center. Today we're going to hear about this."

Pamela turned to Valerie. "What do you remember of the time beneath the truck?"

"Going in and out of consciousness," Valerie answered. "When I wasn't there at the wreck I was in a peaceful room. Like a waiting area." Valerie smiled. "I wanted to stay there."

"Heaven." Pamela paused. "What is heaven like? You told me you saw a great feast there. Maybe the Wedding Supper of the Lamb mentioned in Revelation."

"Yes. I saw my daughters there. They were sitting at the table with many others. I wasn't a participant, though…just more of an onlooker."

"And you saw Jesus." Pamela asked the question everyone was waiting to hear. "What is Jesus like?"

"He is powerful…and He hums. But Jesus is also gentle. I saw passion in His eyes, and it was for me. But Jesus is also humble. It was His innocence that really gripped me. And He was telling me with every fiber of His being that He loved me."

Valerie cleared her throat, overwhelmed by remembering. "It's hard to explain…" she tried to continue. "I looked at Him and thought, 'How could they have hurt Him…killed Him?'"

Finding it difficult to look into the camera, Valerie said, "Then I thought, I killed Him. He was wounded for my transgressions. And…I think I understood…I'm sure for the first time ever…that Jesus loves all of us. He loves His creation purely. He's not a man. He's God. That kind of love is wholly His."

The camera was steady as Valerie composed herself. "I know," she continued with less difficulty, "that if I had been the only person trapped in sin and self-hatred, Jesus loves me so much He would've died for me alone.

"I'm just so glad I died."

The Bride of Christ

As Valerie's spirit returned fully to her body and Jesus declared, "This is My beloved Bride," she understood the metaphor to mean that she was a picture of today's Church—those who call Jesus, the Son of God, their Savior and Lord.

Jesus loves His Bride, even though she is fractured and not yet manifesting what He prayed for her in John 17. There, Jesus asked the Father to unite His followers, making them one as Jesus, the Father, and the Spirit are one. The Church is not there yet. There is more to do before she is the flawless Bride Jesus will retrieve.

This was the restoration Valerie, Cheryl, and the other intercessors prayed for prior to the accident. Their prayers were rooted in centuries of biblical history. At first, only Israel was God's betrothed. God described the relationship through His prophet, Isaiah:

For your Maker is your husband, the Lord of hosts is his name; and the Holy One of Israel is your Redeemer, the God of the whole earth he is called. For the Lord has called you like a wife deserted and grieved in spirit, like a wife of youth when she is cast off, says your God (Isaiah 54:5–6).

God's love for His betrothed is sweet and strong:

You shall no more be termed Forsaken, and your land shall no more be termed Desolate, but you shall be called My Delight Is in Her, and your land Married; for the Lord delights in you, and your land shall be married. For as a young man marries a young woman, so shall your sons marry you, and as the bridegroom rejoices over the bride, so shall your God rejoice over you (Isaiah 62:4–5).

The prophet Hosea described a time when the children of Israel would be wedded to God in eternity:

And in that day, declares the Lord, you will call me "My Husband," and no longer will you call me "My Baal." For I will remove the names of the Baals from her mouth, and they shall be remembered by name no more. And I will make for them a covenant on that day with the beasts of the field, the birds of the heavens, and the creeping things of the ground. And I will abolish the bow, the sword, and war from the land, and I will make you lie down in safety. And I will betroth you to me forever. I will betroth you to me in righteousness and in justice, in steadfast love and in mercy. I will betroth you to me in faithfulness. And you shall know the Lord (Hosea 2:16–20).

Verse 23 mentions those who are not Jews, yet become God's people by accepting Christ. "And I will have mercy on No Mercy, and I will say to Not My People, 'You are my people'...."

God's love is perfect, but His people have not loved Him perfectly. Hosea's life was a living demonstration of that fact. God asked Hosea to marry a prostitute named Gomer. Her unfaithfulness pictured Israel's infidelity to God. Hosea's steadfast love reflected God's love for His wayward people.

Jesus came to show the world that God loves everyone. The New Testament book of Romans reveals that Christians share in Israel's spiritual riches through the death and resurrection of Christ. Those riches can be enjoyed by anyone who chooses Christ as Savior and Lord. The following passage explains how we enter God's family:

> *If you confess with your mouth that Jesus is Lord and believe in your heart that God raised him from the dead, you will be saved. For with the heart one believes and is justified, and with the mouth one confesses and is saved. For the Scripture says, "Everyone who believes in him will not be put to shame." For there is no distinction between Jew and Greek; the same Lord is Lord of all, bestowing his riches on all who call on him. For "everyone who calls on the name of the Lord will be saved"* (Romans 10:9–11, emphasis added).

Writing to the church at Corinth, the apostle Paul spoke of Christ and His Bride, saying: *"I betrothed you to one husband, to present you as a pure virgin to Christ"* (2 Cor. 11:2). In his letter to the Ephesians, Paul explained what Christ did for His Bride and how she is to reflect Him:

Christ loved the church and gave himself up for her, that he might sanctify her, having cleansed her by the washing of water with the word, so that he might present the church to himself in splendor, without spot or wrinkle or any such thing, that she might be holy and without blemish (Ephesians 5:25–27).

Just as Christ made Valerie whole and continues recreating her mind, will, and emotions, He also leads His Church to wholeness.

The Bridegroom loves His Bride. In John chapter 14, Jesus promised to return and take her to His Father's house. The promise reflects ancient custom. A betrothed man was given a year to prepare a home for his bride. She was to remain pure and alert, expecting his return at any moment.

Christ promises that He is a faithful Bridegroom preparing a wonderful home for His Bride, the Church. One day, perhaps when we least expect it, He will come and take us home! Meanwhile, we can wait in hope, trusting Him.

Let not your hearts be troubled. Believe in God; believe also in me. In my Father's house are many rooms. If it were not so, would I have told you that I go to prepare a place for you? And if I go and prepare a place for you, I will come again and will take you to myself, that where I am you may be also (John 14:1–3).

As with many weddings, there will be a great feast when Christ returns. It is the Marriage Supper of the Lamb. His Bride will be glorious, pure and dressed in fine white linen. John described the scene:

> *Then I heard what seemed to be the voice of a great multitude,*
> *like the roar of many waters and like the sound of mighty peals*
> *of thunder, crying out, "Hallelujah! For the Lord our God the*
> *Almighty reigns. Let us rejoice and exult and give him the glory,*
> *for the marriage of the Lamb has come, and his Bride has made*
> *herself ready; it was granted her to clothe herself with fine linen,*
> *bright and pure"—for the fine linen is the righteous deeds of the*
> *saints (Revelation 19:6–8).*

Valerie's shattered state pictured the Church metaphorically. Her healing and restoration serves as encouragement that Jesus *will* work to ready His beloved Bride for His return and for the joys of eternity with Him.

A Work in Progress (Valerie)

Like yours, my story is a work in progress. In returning to my family, I hoped to see my marriage saved. Unfortunately, it did not survive because it did not change. That is not the way I would have planned it. Yet God carried me through the heartache of the divorce.

After my experience with Jesus, my interior landscape was transformed. I don't think it has anything to do with brain damage. What I know now is that I am deeply loved and carefully watched over by Jesus, who knows my every need. This world is not my home, but a precursor to heaven. With a perspective born of experience, I know that eternity is a breath away, and majesty awaits me there.

Fourteen years later, I am still ecstatic about Jesus' love and still blinded by His radiance. He is all I want and all I need. No longer am I insecure. How can I be, when I know how He loves me? He told me so Himself! He knows my name—*Valerie*—and I will hear Him whisper it again.

Each day I am clothed in peace. Because I am more aware of my value to Him, my divorce did not destroy me. My relationship with Ashley remains tender. Her heart is still healing from the horror of the accident. But we relate to one another, and love each other for who we are today.

Prior to the accident, fear drove me and made too many decisions for me. It is ironic: death is often our greatest fear, but it has become my greatest expectation. That doesn't leave much for me to be afraid of.

If I am tempted to fret, I look up. To say I have never worried would be untruthful. But I am different. When people tell me that, I know what they mean. The old me pretended there was no self-doubt behind the façade of laughter and sarcasm. But there was. I was a pleaser who never felt "good enough."

Those days are over. The old Valerie died in a mangled silver Jeep. The new Valerie is secure in the Savior's love. I don't have to work at; I simply receive it. That is the love I want to share—the love of the heavenly Groom for His Bride.

To share it with those who struggle as I once did—that is my hope. My life isn't perfect. Perfection is not possible in this broken world. But for those who know Jesus, there is a joy that exceeds all imagination. Its fullness waits on the other side of our last moment on Earth, yet we can experience joy here.

Yes. Jesus came to give us abundant life even *now*.

Ashley, Valerie, and Elissa (Easter 2010)

Note

1. Excerpts of interview segments: "A Modern Day Resurrection," from the program, Ravished Heart (June 2010), hosted by Pamela Carter, http://www.xpmedia.com/channel/pcarter/video/2. (Some excerpts have been paraphrased.)

13

A BEAUTIFUL STORY

There is a beautiful story from ancient times that reveals the heart of Christ. It is a story of resurrection and life. The story is not uplifting at first. It begins with suffering, followed by death and deep sorrow. The usual questions come up—the human reflexes that ask, "Why?" and "What if?"

Everyone can relate to the characters in this story. Everyone has suffered losses and asked the same questions. As you read the account, remember that it really happened, days before Jesus' own death and resurrection.

Both stories have been recorded *for you.*

Lazarus Comes Forth[1]

On a difficult morning in Bethany, Mary held her brother's ashen hand. How could someone so robust deteriorate so quickly? Mary's eyes wandered toward the orchard outside where Lazarus loved pruning his precious vines.

The nightmare started the day before. By evening, their brother went to bed, drenched from fever and too weak to stand. Martha offered him fresh soup. He never ate it. He could not keep anything down. Mary remained at her brother's side. *What if he needs something and I'm not there?*

Martha paced the living room, then brought her brother unleavened cakes and wine. *Maybe these will be appealing.* But Lazarus was beyond eating. He was dying and the sisters knew it. Sickness had come unexpectedly to cut him down.

"If only Jesus were here," said Mary. "He'd heal our brother."

"Can't we send our neighbor, Benjamin, to find Him?" Martha seemed hopeful.

"I'm not sure there is time, Martha. Look how shallow his breathing is."

Martha had already run from the room. She was sure Jesus would come. Every time the Rabbi came through Bethany, He and His friends stayed with their family and ate the special dishes Martha prepared for them. Lazarus made everyone laugh, especially Jesus. After dinner the conversation would become more serious. Mary would listen as Jesus talked about *the Father*. Martha usually did the dishes. Still, she heard what Jesus said. She knew this man of God loved her.

He will come when He hears about our brother.

"Benjamin! Benjamin!" she cried as she ran.

"What is it, Martha?"

"Please go find Jesus, the Rabbi!" She was out of breath. "Lazarus is sick. Dying, I'm afraid. Tell Jesus that He must come now or it will be too late."

Benjamin had no idea where the Rabbi was. Finally, he found someone who could take the message to Jesus. The messenger was fervent: "Lord, the one You love is ill. You must go to Bethany and heal Your brother, Lazarus."

Jesus knew about the trouble in Bethany. "This sickness won't end in death," He assured the man. "What's happening there is for God's glory. You'll see."

Relieved to hear the good news, the messenger carried it back to Bethany. But it was too late. Lazarus had died, and Jesus never showed up. *Didn't He say this sickness would not end in death?*

Two days later, Jesus said to His friends, "Let's go to Judea."

"We can't do that," they warned. "The Jewish leaders wanted to stone You the last time we went near Jerusalem! Why risk such danger now?"

"I have come to Earth to do a job. We all work when it's light. Right now, it's light for Me." Jesus words were cryptic. "Our friend Lazarus has fallen asleep, but I am going to wake him up."

"If he's sleeping, he'll be okay," rationalized the disciples.

"Lazarus is dead," Jesus explained. "And for your sakes I'm glad I wasn't there. You are about to see something you wouldn't believe." Jesus reached for His tunic and sandals. "Let's go to him."

Thomas looked around at the others. "Let's go to him…and die with him."

Bethany was only two miles from Jerusalem, and many Jews from the city were gathered when Jesus and the disciples arrived.

"Jesus is coming, Martha," whispered Benjamin, who had seen the Rabbi pass his home.

Jesus was waiting in the vineyard when Martha ran to meet Him. She had rehearsed what she would say to the Rabbi, and she threw herself at Him, crying, "If only You'd been here, Lazarus wouldn't have died! But even now You could ask God and He will give You whatever You want."

"Your brother will live again." Jesus said.

Martha could not imagine what He meant by that. Was He being theological? *Lazarus is in heaven. Small comfort when Jesus could have healed him here on the earth.* "I know he will rise again in the resurrection of the last day. Is that what you mean?"

"I am the resurrection and the life. Whoever believes in Me will live even if he dies, and everyone who lives and believes in Me will never die." Jesus made Martha look Him in the eyes. "Do you believe it's true?"

Piercing, His eyes demanded an answer. "Yes, Lord. I believe You are the Christ. You are the Son of God." It was not the answer He was looking for. But she would see.

"Where's Mary?" asked Jesus.

"I'll go get her." Martha wiped her wet cheeks and ran to the house.

"Mary," she whispered to her sister. "Jesus is in the vineyard. He is asking for you."

Mary leapt up and ran. The grievers followed her, thinking she was planning to wail at her brother's tomb. But they saw Jesus waiting for Mary. They watched as He listened to her sorrow.

"Lord, if You'd only been here Lazarus wouldn't have died!" she cried.

Oh, He loved her. He loved them all. Her grief became His. She could not know what He would do. She only knew that He asked too much when He allowed her brother to die.

This was why He asked Martha whether she believed—not in some theological idea about Messiah. No. Did she believe He *loved* her and knew her needs? Did she believe He could be trusted to do what only God can do?

Did she believe that God is good? That was the question everyone had missed.

"Where did you bury him?" Jesus asked.

"Lord, come and see."

Jesus cried, feeling the pain death brings. Death is not what the Trinity planned from the beginning. But there it was. And in a few short days, the scene would play out again, in Jesus' own life. There would be a death and a resurrection, so those who died could live.

"See how much he loved Lazarus!" mused some of the Jews. "He's crying with Mary and Martha."

"If He can open the eyes of the blind, surely He could've kept this man from dying," murmured others. "I doubt He loved him that much or He would have been here."

The tomb was a cave. At the entrance sat an enormous rock. "Remove that stone," said Jesus.

Martha touched the Rabbi's arm. "Lord, he's been dead four days. He stinks by now."

"Didn't I tell you that if you believe you'll see the glory of God?" *Maybe she'll finally understand.*

They took away the stone.

Jesus looked up to heaven. "Father, I know You always hear Me, but I speak for the sake of these people. I want them to believe that You sent Me."

What He did next was beyond anything they could have believed. "Lazarus, Come here!"

No one moved…or breathed. *Will he come out of the tomb? He's been dead four days!*

Still bound in grave clothes and smelling of death, Lazarus stumbled from his grave.

"Unbind him. Let him go!" Jesus ordered.

Lazarus went from death to life. Had Jesus talked with him beforehand? Had He asked the man whether he was willing to die for his Lord? Clearly, his death and resurrection were part of the plan.

The story spread like wildfire. "Jesus brings dead man back to life." It made the religious folks mad enough to kill Jesus, if only to keep the crowds from calling Him Messiah. Yet they could not stop what people believed, because in a few days, Jesus rolled away His own stone and left His own grave clothes behind.

Jesus asked no more of Lazarus than He expected of Himself. *Everything*, for the sake of life—abundant, overflowing, perfect, eternal life.

Not much is known about Lazarus' second life. We know Jesus sat with the family for one last meal. Mary broke open a bottle of perfume that cost as much as a year's wages, and poured it onto Jesus' feet. She wept as she rubbed it into His skin. Then she wiped away the excess with her hair. No price was too great to express her gratitude. Her brother was alive and well. Lazarus watched as she thanked their Lord.

At some point, Lazarus' earthly body died again. This time, he went to be with Jesus forever. He was a different man from the one first buried. No doubt he shared his story of Jesus' love, and of how it changed him, before he died again.

So it is with Valerie. Life on Earth is still life on Earth. But it is not life as usual. On the day Jesus asked whether she was willing to die for Him, she could not have known all it would mean. Yet she has no regrets. Like Martha, she was asked to believe that Jesus loves her…enough to raise her from the dead or keep her in heaven. Either way His love is real, and even in death, she lives.

For Jesus and heaven are but a breath away.

Note

1. Story is based on the Gospel of John, chapter 11.

AFTERWORD: THE BOOK

On a Sunday in 2001, at Christian Life Center in Riverside, California, I saw a lovely dark-haired lady sitting next to Jane Lankhorst, our pastor's wife. An unusual light was blinking from the woman's dark sunglasses. It got my attention.

Our congregation had prayed for Valerie Paters since her car wreck in March of the previous year. I knew this must be Valerie. Sitting next to her was a pretty woman I assumed to be her sister, Cheryl Schuelke. Jack and Jane Lankhorst had pastored the sisters at Canyon Chapel Church in Flagstaff, Arizona and remained their close friends.

Early in the service, Jane introduced Valerie and Cheryl to the congregation, and had Cheryl briefly tell about the wreck and about Valerie's progress. I don't remember them speaking of heaven at the time. Jane told me later that Valerie had an amazing encounter with Christ during her three days on life support.

I didn't see Cheryl again until 2005 when she and I were part of a mission my church had undertaken in Cambodia. During a bus ride, she told me the whole story of Valerie's encounter in heaven. She also said they were praying to find a writer to help them with a book.

"I am a published author," I ventured. "Maybe I could help you with it."

"Let's pray about it," Cheryl replied. "We want to make sure we find the right person."

"Me, too," I answered with some relief. "I'd almost have to experience what Valerie did just to write it. I'd have to believe it, too."

Not long after returning from Cambodia, Cheryl and Valerie returned to Riverside. My husband and I invited them, Jack, and Jane over for dinner. I had the privilege of hearing Valerie tell the story in her own words. *If this is all true, it's the most stunning account of heaven I've ever heard.*

Valerie reiterated their hopes for a writer to adequately convey not only the story, but the heart of Christ's love. Would I let them read *Lisa*, my first book?

In March of 2010 we connected again, through Facebook. Here is part of Cheryl's message:

> *It's been a long time since I've talked to you. Are you interested in possibly writing my sister Valerie's story? I remember when we first talked about the possibility in Cambodia and we prayed about it. Also remember praying at your home later in that year. The Lord is saying to us, "It is time." Everywhere Valerie goes people want to know if she has a book.*

Though I said I would be interested, it was almost a year before we set a time. Cheryl and Valerie arrived in Huntington Beach, California, for a long weekend in November 2011 so we could take as much time as we needed to record the story and backstories of the wreck and heaven.

I still was praying about whether I really could write with the passion Valerie's experience deserved. Cheryl and Valerie are authentic Christian women. They related their story with earnestness and great detail. My prayer beforehand was that God would give me assurances that I was the one to put it on paper.

"What happened when you first saw Christ?" I asked.

"I turned around to be swept up in nearly overwhelming brightness," Valerie replied. "It pulled me into it. There in its midst was Jesus. 'It's You!' I exclaimed. I touched His face. 'It's really You.'"

"What did He do then?" I asked, mesmerized.

"He spread His arms out wide, gesturing as He spoke to me. 'Valerie, don't you know how much I love you?' When He spoke there was this iridescence in the air." Valerie reached into her purse and pulled out a piece of gift-wrapping ribbon that she carries with her. It is the color of an opal, reflecting pastel light.

"Like this," she said, handing me the ribbon.

She didn't have to show me. I'd seen that gem-charged air once before, on the day of my mother's funeral.

Because of the cancer that stole her health, Mother's death was hard. Though I lived a couple of hours away, I made the drive to spend one day each week with her. Toward the end of her journey, we talked mostly of heaven. She was sure the journey would be lonely. "I'll miss you more than you miss me, Kay."

"No, Mother. I'm pretty sure He'll be all you need. But if there is some way to let me know you are in heaven, please communicate it somehow." I choked up. "Maybe Jesus would let me see that you are all right."

We held hands for a bit and cried over missing one another, before it happened. Then we went inside to pick out the clothes Mother would wear for her funeral.

The afternoon heat in Fort Worth, Texas is oppressive in August. But after Mother's burial, I wandered to the back porch of her home anyway. I didn't want to see the people bustling in her kitchen. That was *her* joy—bustling.

The cushions were hot as I settled into one of the redwood chairs. It was odd not having my mother beside me. I took a deep breath and was about to look out over the garden when my mother's face appeared before me, radiant with an iridescence that sparkled like tiny diamonds.

"It's all right, precious. It's all right."

My heart pounded in my chest. Then she said it again, "It's all right, precious. It's all right." Devoid of its former pain, her face glowed in its current joy. It hung there a moment longer, and was gone.

Tears of relief and thankfulness poured down my face. She was home. And Jesus had let me see her the way He did. But He also let me see what Valerie saw—the atmosphere of heaven sparkling like the bow on a bridal gift.

I knew then that I could write Valerie's story.

—**Kay Farish**

AFTERGLOW

Life since my return from heaven hasn't been easy. My physical health continues to be a work in progress. Although I have exceeded the expectations of the medical community, I know wholeness is something I can only achieve through the ultimate Healer—body, mind, and soul—and so I seek God.

All these years later, I still have a deep longing for heaven. I continue to feel out of place here on earth and homesick for my eternal home. But my spiritual bond with my sister Cheryl helps sustain me. And God's spirit continues to comfort me, allowing me to have peace in this life until I get to go to my true home again.

My sister and I continue to feel that connection to heaven daily. Especially in our nightly dreams, heaven exists as a vivid reminder of our eternal home. I recount my dreams by memory, but Cheryl captures her dreams in a journal, documenting each treasured memory as an assurance that God will bring us to His glorious home one day.

But the most important thing for Cheryl and me is our prayer life. We relish it. I make myself available to listen to God and have found that I bond with God the best while sitting in my recliner in the family room. There, I read the Word, meditate, ask questions of God, and listen for His voice. I have actually had guests sit in my "special" chair and say, "Is this where you meet with God? I can feel His presence here."

Cheryl also seeks God in special places like her backyard garden, her bedroom, or anywhere else she can be alone with Him.

Cheryl and I have always approached prayer by asking what is on the Father's heart and how He would have His children pray. There are many things we can pray, but what is it that is pressing in on His heart for this specific moment? We continue to ask that question and try to carry on a sort of continual prayer fellowship in our ministry, serving as intercessors in Heart to Heart, our prayer group at church.

I know I came back for a purpose. Before Jesus sent me back to earth, He told me, "Tell them who I am; tell them how much I love them." It was my great commission. Today, Cheryl and I are blessed to share our testimony, nationally and internationally, of the wonders of heaven and Jesus's great love for each of us. That is what I came back to share: Jesus's desire is for you to know that you are loved deeply and carefully watched over by Him. He knows your every need. He pursues you with His passionate love. My prayer now and always is you may know and experience the depths of His love.

Always remember that prayer is key. Prayer is relational, prayer is powerful, and prayer brings heaven to earth! I pray that you will continually abide in the Father and know His unconditional love.

A MOTHER'S HOPE

by Tiffini Dingman-Grover

Something was wrong with my son David. He was a big kid, eight years old, 150 pounds, but he had lost his appetite. He'd stopped telling jokes, too, stopped being his usual happy-go-lucky self. His jaw hurt for no discernible reason. He began throwing up. We thought David was suffering side effects from his medication for attention-deficit disorder. Then he threw up in the car on the way to his favorite restaurant, and the pediatrician told us to get him to a hospital immediately. The emergency-room doctor was young, a resident. He checked David over, shined a light down his throat. He was so shocked by what he saw, he uttered something I can't repeat in polite company. The doctor apologized and said, "We need an MRI immediately." I noticed the nurse crying. What did she know that I didn't? Hours later, at 2:00 AM, I found out. The diagnosis was still imprecise, but David was being admitted. To the oncology ward. "A massive growth is pushing into your son's throat," the doctor said.

"Mommy, what's wrong with me?" David asked.

"You're going to be okay, sweetheart."

"You'll make it go away, right, Mommy?"

"Of course I will."

They gave David pain medication, and he soon fell asleep. My husband, Bryn, and I lay on the floor. The room had a recliner chair, but neither of us could figure out how to work it. My mother-in-law had already taken our two older boys, Matthew and Keith, home. In the dark, I tried to pray. But all that came at first were memories.

David was our youngest child, our baby. I loved him more than I knew it was possible to love anyone. We had a good-night ritual we went through, no matter what kind of day it had been. I would say, "You." He would say, "Me." And together we would say, "Forever. Sleep with the angels, roses on the pillow, sleep with Jesus."

You, me, forever. Lying on that cold hospital floor, I felt fear and anger build. Twice before David, I had gotten pregnant, only to lose the babies. *God, You didn't give me David just to take him away, did You?* A piece of medical equipment beeped. *Can You at least give me some kind of answer? Some reassurance?* Silence. I waited in that silence a long time. No answer came. *Fine,* I finally decided. *I'll do it myself.* David was going to live. No power on earth would take my boy from me.

David did have cancer, in one of the worst places possible, at the base of his skull. His particular cancer was called rhabdomyosarcoma, an aggressive tumor spreading across much of the left side of his face and pressing on his carotid artery and optical nerve. It was why his jaw had hurt and he had felt so sick. It also explained his mood swings. The tumor was right next to his brain. So close, in fact, that surgery was out of the question. David's only chance was intensive chemotherapy and radiation. Even then, only half of kids diagnosed with his kind of cancer survived five years.

Those odds didn't daunt me. I was determined to will David back to health. Bryn and I both worked for a computer software company—I handled finances, Bryn managed the warehouse—and our bosses generously allowed us to take time off and work odd shifts to spend as many days and nights with David as possible. We became his nurses, his coaches, his constant companions. He had an IV line inserted in his chest. We learned how to clean it and check for infection. His eyes developed nystagmus from the pressure on the optical nerve. We made certain his patch stayed in place. When he had trouble breathing, we held the oxygen mask to his mouth.

As David's treatment advanced, doctors told Bryn and me that his chances were even worse than most kids'. The cancer was too deeply entrenched. I refused to be discouraged. Although the chemotherapy left David skinny and weak, I urged him out of bed every day to walk down the hall.

We reached our insurance company's one-million-dollar coverage cap in eleven months. After that, we faced bills up to fourteen hundred dollars a week. *Not going to stop us*, I thought. I began selling off clothes and other things around the house. Much later, when we learned that only an expensive experimental surgery had a chance of saving David, I even went on eBay and put up for auction one of the "Frank Must Die" bumper stickers Bryn had made—"Frank" was our family nickname for David's cancer, short for Frankenstein. I told potential bidders I was trying to raise money for my son's cancer care. Amazingly, we got some media coverage—a reporter at our small hometown paper happened to know someone at the *Washington Post*—and money came in. The support was wonderful. Still, David wasn't getting any better.

One night in the hospital, he sat up in bed and said, "Mom, the angels came to talk to me. It's time for me to go."

I peered at him through the dimness, fighting to stay calm. Was he dreaming? "You saw angels, David?"

"They're here with me now, Mom. It's time to go. I'm tired."

I struggled to control my voice. "Sweetheart, I know you're tired. But you're not ready to go. Fight. Stay with me. Just stay with me a little while longer."

I rushed out of the room and told the nurses, then called Bryn and asked him to gather everyone. I was about to start praying when a nurse came up to me. "Tiffini, I'm sorry. David's vital signs are very low. This could be the end. We've done everything we can for him. His little body is worn out."

I went back to David's room and sat in a chair in the dark. Again, my fear surged and I felt it form into words. I started to pray, then stopped. Something pressed on me, some resistance. God? Or just my own exhaustion? I was deeply tired. Tired of fighting. Tired of

206 | **Heaven Is a Breath Away**

fruitless hope. *Why, God? Why? He's mine. You can't take him!* Again the pressure, the resistance. Only this time it had a shape, almost like a blanket settling over me. A calmness, a sense of release. I heard words: *David is a gift. Love him. Don't own him.* The calmness deepened, and I found myself repeating that word, *gift.* I had been trying so hard, throwing every ounce of strength into David's life. What if that life wasn't mine to have, to direct according to my will? What if the best thing I could do for David was give him to God? *Lord, David's life is a gift from You, not me. Let Your will be done.*

I looked up. Our entire family was there. They kissed David and said good-bye. When they left, Bryn and I sat together in the room, holding each other, crying and praying. We didn't stop until 7:00 AM, when David suddenly sat up. We looked at the monitors. His vital signs were normal.

"What are you guys doing?" he asked.

"David? Are you all right?" I asked.

"Um, yeah."

"Can you remember anything at all about last night?"

David cocked his head. "You mean about Jesus? Sure. He told me I could stay awhile longer. There's more for me to do."

"You...talked to Jesus? Did you actually see Him?"

David made a face. "Mom, come on. He was too bright. I could only see the angels. They were gold."

"But you feel okay?" I asked.

"Yes, I feel fine."

Today David is a challenging thirteen-year-old. The road has not been easy. Radiation and chemotherapy did not rid him of cancer. We ended up taking him to Los Angeles for an experimental surgery that removed nearly all of his tumor.

Sometimes I think of the anger I felt that awful first night in the emergency room, my fist-shaking on the cold hospital floor. I don't blame myself for it. I'm a mother, after all. And I suppose I needed to pass through that anger to learn the lesson of my son's illness. As is common with kids who survive cancer, David lives with side effects from radiation and surgery. He has good days and bad days. Yet he and I both know that each and every day is a gift. And that it is a blessing to say each night, "You, me, forever."

A Note from the Editors

We hope you enjoy *Heaven Is a Breath Away* by Valerie Paters and Cheryl Schuelke with Kay Farish, specially selected by the editors of the Books and Inspirational Media Division of Guideposts, a nonprofit organization that touches millions of lives every day through products and services that inspire, encourage, help you grow in your faith, and celebrate God's love in every aspect of your daily life.

Thank you for making a difference with your purchase of this book, which helps fund our many outreach programs to military personnel, prisons, hospitals, nursing homes, and educational institutions. To learn more, visit GuidepostsFoundation.org.

We also maintain many useful and uplifting online resources. Visit Guideposts.org to read true stories of hope and inspiration, access OurPrayer network, sign up for free newsletters, download free e-books, join our Facebook community, and follow our stimulating blogs.

To learn about other Guideposts publications, including the best-selling devotional *Daily Guideposts*, go to ShopGuideposts .org, call (800) 932-2145, or write to Guideposts, PO Box 5815, Harlan, Iowa 51593.